Satyam

The Eternal Tr...

Dr. Venkat Potana

Price: $ 20
All Proceeds support Mission work:
To pay via Author's zelle: send to
pothanav@gmail.com or +1(469)-332-0026

Copyright

© 2025 by Dr. Venkat Potana
All rights reserved.

No part of this publication may be reproduced, stored in a retrieval system, or transmitted in any form or by any means electronic, mechanical, photocopying, recording, or otherwise without the prior written permission of the publisher, except for brief quotations used in critical reviews or scholarly works.

Pothana Publications — An independent imprint of the author
Dallas, Texas, USA
Email: potanabooks@gmail.com

Title: Satyam Shivam Christam: *The Eternal Truth in Hinduism and Christianity*
ISBN: **9798274262231**
Printed in the United States of America.

Disclaimer
　　This book is written and published solely for educational, intercultural, and philosophical study. It is not intended to promote, convert, or persuade readers toward any particular faith, belief, or religious practice. The material represents the author's personal reflections and comparative observations between classical Hindu and Christian philosophical thought.
　　All interpretations and conclusions expressed herein are subjective opinions of the author, presented for the reader's own study and discernment. The reader is fully free to agree, disagree, or interpret differently.
　　Neither the author nor the publisher makes any absolute religious, historical, or legal claims and shall not be held responsible for how the contents of this book are interpreted, used, or applied. All scriptural and literary citations from Hindu or Christian texts are used respectfully and for academic and reflective purposes only.
　　The intent of this publication is to foster mutual understanding, peace, and scholarly dialogue among readers of diverse cultural and spiritual backgrounds. Any resemblance to doctrinal assertion or religious exclusivity is unintentional and should not be construed as proselytism.

Quotations from the Vedas are primarily taken from *The Rig Veda: An Anthology*, translated by **Wendy Doniger O'Flaherty** (Penguin Classics, 1981). Supplementary references are drawn from **Ralph T. H. Griffith's** English translations of *The Sama Veda, The Yajur Veda*, and *The Atharva Veda* (originally published 1889–1899; reprinted by Motilal Banarsidass).

Biblical quotations are taken from the **Holy Bible, New International Version (NIV)**

All efforts have been made to ensure textual accuracy and faithful representation of both Sanskrit and Biblical sources for comparative and contemplative study.

About the Author

Dr. Venkat Potana is a pastor, theologian, missiologist, professor, and author with more than 30 years of ministry experience across India and the United States. He holds a Ph.D. in Theology and Missiology and additional advanced qualifications in intercultural studies, philosophy, social work, and divinity. Besides that, he has trained and mentored thousands of students, pastors, and leaders in several nations in different contexts. Presently, he lives in Dallas and holds a religious visa to work with TEEM International, where he mentors couples, equips church leaders, and travels extensively as an itinerant evangelist.

Dr. Potana has written 45-plus books in the areas of theology, missions, family, and discipleship (they are all available on Amazon.com). His books address practical topics of concern such as indigenous missions, college students as target for outreach, parenting, and marriage; and he also writes in the academic realm, publishing articles in peer-reviewed journals and presenting at international conferences. He has appeared on CBN and other television networks presenting his testimony, reflecting on cultural issues, and presenting his ministry engage in culturally contextualized ministries.

Beyond academia and writing, Dr. Potana's life is devoted to mentoring the next generation and strengthening families and churches. He lives in Dallas, Texas, with his wife Rita and their son, Ashish. His daughters, Sophia and Lydia, are undergraduate BS Nursing students at Hardin Simmons University, Abilene. Together, their family embodies a testimony of faith, mission, and Christ-centered service.

Dedication

To my Lord and Savior, Jesus Christ,
who saved me from the power of sin and death and called me into His marvelous light.
It is by His grace that I stand, not merely as one redeemed, but as a witness of His transforming love and unfailing mercy.

To the One who lifted me from weakness and raised me to serve,
as a pastor, theologian, missionary, scholar, and teacher of His Word

I dedicate this work as an offering of gratitude and devotion.
May every page reflect His power, every word exalt His name,
and every reader encounter His presence through the miracles of Scripture.

All glory to Jesus Christ,
the Author of my salvation and the Sustainer of my calling.

— **Dr. Venkat Potana**

About the Book

In this profound and beautifully written work, Dr. Venkat Potana invites readers on a journey through the spiritual landscapes of Hinduism and Christianity, exploring how the timeless quest for truth, goodness, and divine presence finds its fullest harmony in the revelation of Christ. Blending the insight of a theologian, the depth of a philosopher, and the heart of a seeker, this book presents a rare synthesis of devotional warmth and academic precision.

Satyam Shivam Christam reveals the radiant connections between the Vedas, Upanishads, Bhagavad Gita, and the Bible with clarity and reverence. Each chapter unfolds like a dialogue between two ancient traditions that have shaped humanity's understanding of God and the purpose of life. The author leads readers through the Vedic hymns of creation, the vision of the eternal Word, the longing of the human heart for the divine, and the fulfillment of that longing in the living Christ, who embodies eternal truth and perfect love.

With its poetic language, rich scholarship, and contemplative rhythm, this book appeals to thinkers, believers, and seekers alike. It serves as an illuminating bridge between faith and philosophy, history and revelation, India's spiritual heritage and the Gospel's transforming message. Readers will discover that truth, when sought with sincerity, always leads to light, and that the essence of both traditions points toward a single divine reality of grace and peace.

Dr. Potana's writing speaks to the heart while engaging the mind. Every page reflects reverence for India's sacred wisdom and admiration for the revelation of Christ as the Eternal Word. The book uplifts the reader into a realm of spiritual reflection, offering insight, harmony, and inspiration for those who desire to understand how divine truth transcends all boundaries of culture and language.

Scholarly, meditative, and profoundly moving, ***Satyam Shivam Christam*** is a landmark contribution to the study of comparative theology and interfaith dialogue. It invites every reader to behold the beauty of divine truth as it shines through the songs of the Vedas and the light of the Gospels, revealing one eternal source of love that unites all seekers across time and tradition.

Epigraph

In the Spirit of Bhakta Pothana

When dawn first whispered across the void,
Truth stirred the silence with living flame.
From depths unseen the Light emerged,
And life awoke to praise His name.

The Vedas sang of hidden fire,
Of breath that kindles heart and sky.
The sages heard the Eternal Word,
And bowed before the Mystery high.

Through lotus hearts and rivers pure,
Flowed longing's song from age to age.
In love the Infinite drew near,
To dwell with man and turn the page.

Now shines the Light no night can veil,
The Word made flesh, the world's delight.
In Satyam, Shivam, Christam one,
The soul beholds the Eternal Light.

—Dr. Venkat Potana

Contents

Copyright .... *ii*
About the Author .... *iv*
Dedication .... *v*
About the Book .... *vi*
Epigraph .... *vii*
Contents .... *viii*
Foreword .... *xi*
Preface .... *xiii*
Prologue .... *xv*

Introduction 1

Part I — The Quest for the Eternal
Chapter 1: The Human Heart Seeks the Eternal 6
  1.1 The Universal Search for the Eternal 6
  1.2 The Voice of Wonder in the Vedas 8
  1.3 The Inner Witness (Ātman – आत्मन्) 12
  1.4 The Hunger for Incarnation: The Divine Draws Near 14
    Conclusion: The Eternal Revealed in Christ 17
Chapter 2: The Eternal Word in Every Age 19
  2.1. The Mystery of the Divine Word (Vāk – वाक्) 19
  2.2 The Word as Revelation 22
  2.3 The Word as Creation and Order 24
  2.4 The Word in the Human Heart 27
  2.5 The Universal Vision of the Divine Word 29
    Conclusion: The Eternal Word Revealed in History 31
Chapter 3: The Signs of the Eternal in Creation 33
  3.1. Nature as the Language of the Divine 34
  3.2. Fire – The Sacred Element 37
  3.3. Rivers and Water – Life and Flow 38
  3.4. Light – Illumination and Presence 39
  3.5. The Rhythm and Harmony of Creation 41
  3.6. Creation as a Mirror of the Human Heart 42
  3.7. The Presence of God in Gentle Ways 43
  3.8. Lessons from Creation 44
    Conclusion: The Whisper of the Eternal 46

Part II — The Glimmers of Truth
Chapter 4 Shadows of the Eternal 50

4.1 Dharma – The Path of Righteous Living 51
4.2 Satya – Truth as Guiding Light 52
4.3 Ahimsa – Reverence for Life 54
4.4 The Role of Virtues in Human Formation 55
4.5 Festivals, Rituals, and Ethical Reminder 57
4.6 Shadows in Nature and Daily Life 58
4.7 Yearning for the Personal and Relational God 59
4.8 Moral Intuition as a Guide 60
4.9 Shadows as Preparation for Revelation 61
    Conclusion: Living in the Light of What is Coming 63

Part III — The Fullness Revealed in Christ
Chapter 5: The Longing for the One Who Saves 66
  5.1 Human Longing as a Reflection of the Eternal 67
  5.2 Divine Intervention in Krishna's Teaching 69
  5.3 Longing for Forgiveness and Transformation 70
  5.4 Divine Love as Invitation, Not Coercion 71
  5.5 Preparing the Heart for Christ 72
  5.6 Human Longing and the Promise of Salvation 73
    Reflection and Invitation 74
Chapter 6: The Eternal Word Becomes Flesh 75
  6.1 The Logos Revealed in History 76
  6.2 Christ as Word and Light 78
  6.3 The Relational Presence of God 79
  6.4 Ethical and Spiritual Formation in the Word Made Flesh ... 80
  6.5 Light and Word in Human Experience 81
  6.6 Fulfillment of the Shadows 82
  6.7 The Word as Life-Giving 83
    Conclusion: Encountering the Eternal in Person 84
Chapter 7: Life, Light, and Love 85
  7.1: Life in Christ – Beyond Mere Existence 85
  7.2 Light of Understanding and Moral Discernment 86
  7.3 Love as the Core of Divine Action 87
  7.4 Integration – Life, Light, and Love in Daily Living 87
    Conclusion: Encountering the Reality the Heart Seeks 88
Chapter 8: The Response of the Heart 89
  8.1 Reflection and Awareness 90
  8.2 Trust and Openness 91
  8.3 Relationship and Communion 92
  8.4 Transformation Through Response 93
    Conclusion: Living the Response of the Heart 93

Part IV — Glimpses in Hindu Scriptures
Chapter 9: Glimpses of the Eternal in Hindu Scriptures 96
9.1 Ethical Ideals as Shadows of God 97
9.3 Philosophical Glimpses of the Eternal 98
9.4 Limitations and Preparation for Fulfillment 99
    Conclusion: From Shadows to Fullness 100

Part V — Living in the Light
Chapter 10: Satyam, Shivam, Christam-Eternal Harmony... 102
10.1 Satyam — Glimpses of Eternal Truth 103
10.2 Shivam — Moral Goodness and Virtue 104
10.3 Christam — Jesus Christ as Fullness 105
10.4 Integrating the Triad in Daily Life 106
10.5 Contemplation and Relational Awareness 107
    Conclusion: Satyam, Shivam, Christam as Life Orientation 109
Chapter 11: Walking in Truth and Love 111
11.1 Ethical Living in the Light of Christ 112
11.2 Love as Action and Presence 113
11.3 Conscience and Moral Discernment 115
11.4 Integrating Truth and Love in Daily Practices 116
11.5 Transformation of Character and Heart 117
11.6 Community and Relational Impact 118
    Conclusion: Life as Walking in Light and Love 120
Chapter 12: Rivers Meet — Harmony and Fulfillment 122
12.1 The River of Longing 123
12.2 The River of Insight 124
12.3 The River of Relational Encounter 125
12.4 Harmony in Daily Life 126
12.5 Rivers Meeting the Ocean — Fulfillment in Christ 127
    Conclusion: Contemplating the Confluence 128

Epilogue 130
Appendices 132

Foreword

There are rare moments in the history of thought when a single book rises beyond its pages and becomes a bridge between civilizations. *Satyam Shivam Christam: The Eternal Truth in Hinduism and Christianity* by Dr. Venkat Potana is such a book. It is more than a work of theology or comparative philosophy; it is a luminous journey through the heart of two of the world's most profound spiritual traditions, revealing that truth, when sought sincerely, always leads to divine light.

Dr. Potana writes with the mastery of a scholar and the tenderness of a saint. His words carry the fragrance of ancient wisdom and the power of divine revelation. Every page reflects deep reverence for India's sacred heritage and radiant faith in the eternal Christ who fulfills every longing of the human soul. The reader does not feel argued with but invited, not instructed but inspired. The tone is gentle, the reasoning precise, and the spiritual insight astonishingly rich.

In this book, Dr. Potana achieves something very few authors have ever done. He honors the Vedic vision with purity of respect while unveiling the fullness of truth in the revelation of Christ. He reads the Vedas, Upanishads, and the Gita with the eyes of devotion and interprets the Gospel with the heart of a pilgrim who has walked through both worlds. The result is a work of rare balance — academically sound, culturally respectful, and spiritually transforming.

Readers will find in *Satyam Shivam Christam* not merely a comparative study but an encounter with the Eternal. The author's prose glows with poetic beauty, his thoughts flow with scriptural harmony, and his insights awaken both wonder and worship. The dialogue he presents between Satyam (Truth), Shivam (Goodness), and Christam (Divine Love) is not theoretical but experiential, leading the reader into personal reflection and revelation.

Every seeker who has ever asked, "Can the wisdom of the East and the light of the Gospel meet in peace?" will find their answer here. This book speaks to the mind of the philosopher, the faith of the theologian, and the devotion of the bhakta. It is both a scholarly contribution and a spiritual treasure, worthy of study, meditation, and lifelong admiration.

Dr. Venkat Potana has given to our generation a masterpiece that will echo through seminaries, temples, churches, and universities for years to come. His vision is global, his devotion is personal, and his voice carries the clarity of one who has seen truth from both sides of the river.

To read *Satyam Shivam Christam* is to walk into the meeting of two great lights — the ancient wisdom of India and the eternal revelation of Christ — and to discover in their harmony the timeless melody of divine love.

This book deserves not only to be read but to be cherished. It stands as a monumental contribution to the study of world spirituality and a living testimony to how faith and philosophy can meet without conflict, revealing the Eternal who transcends all boundaries.

—*Professor Arvind Nath Ramasena, Ph.D.*

Preface

The search for eternal truth is as ancient as humanity itself. Every civilization, every sage, every heart that has looked toward the heavens has felt the same inner longing — a desire to know the source of life, love, and light. India's spiritual heritage has preserved this longing through the songs of the Vedas, the wisdom of the Upanishads, and the devotion of the Bhakti poets. Across the ages, this longing has taken many forms, yet its essence remains one: the yearning to behold the Eternal.

This book was born from that same longing. It began as a quiet reflection during my years of study and ministry across continents, as I encountered seekers from both the East and the West who asked the same timeless questions. What is truth? Who is the Eternal? Can there be harmony between the wisdom of the ancients and the revelation of Christ? I discovered that these questions do not divide us; they unite us. They are the heartbeat of every soul searching for meaning.

Satyam Shivam Christam is not a book of argument or persuasion. It is a journey of discovery, an invitation to reflection. It seeks to listen to the echoes of divine truth in the sacred texts of Hinduism and Christianity and to observe how those echoes lead toward a radiant convergence. The purpose is not to compare but to contemplate, not to prove but to perceive. Every page has been written with reverence for India's spiritual tradition and gratitude for the revelation of Christ as the Eternal Word.

In the process of writing, I felt as though I was walking along the banks of two mighty rivers — the river of India's wisdom and the river of the Gospel's grace. Both arise from the same source, flow through different lands, and finally meet in the ocean of divine love. That meeting place is the vision behind this book. The Sanskrit expressions *Satyam* (Truth) and *Shivam* (Goodness) find their eternal harmony in *Christam* (Divine Anointing). Together, they form the triad of life's highest realization: the truth that enlightens, the goodness that sanctifies, and the love that redeems.

The purpose of this work is to awaken wonder and cultivate respect. The Vedic seers, the Hebrew prophets, and the early Christian apostles all sought the same Eternal who transcends all boundaries of language and culture. The intention of this book is to recognize that shared quest and to reveal how the light of Christ fulfills, without negating, the longings of the human spirit expressed throughout history.

Throughout these pages, the reader will encounter a gentle dialogue — not between religions, but between hearts that seek understanding. The wisdom of the East and the revelation of the West are presented not as rivals but as companions in the search for truth. Each reflection is offered with humility, shaped by scholarship, and carried by devotion.

As I place this work before you, I do so with a prayerful hope. May it inspire reflection, deepen faith, and open new paths of dialogue among those who love truth. May it serve scholars who desire precision, seekers who long for meaning, and believers who wish to see how divine grace moves across every culture and generation. Above all, may every reader sense the eternal presence of God — the One who speaks through the stars, the scriptures, and the silence of the soul.

To all who walk this path of discovery, may your journey through *Satyam Shivam Christam* bring peace to the mind, light to the heart, and reverence to the spirit. For in every sincere search for truth, the Eternal is already near.

—*Dr. Venkat Potana*
Dallas, Texas

Prologue

Across the ages, humanity has lifted its eyes toward the heavens in search of the Eternal. Every civilization has asked the same sacred questions: What is truth? What gives meaning to life? Who is the source of all that exists? Within this longing lies the story of every heart that seeks the living God.

India's ancient wisdom carries a remarkable record of this search. The Vedic hymns and Upanishadic meditations reveal the human desire to know the unseen Creator, to find light that never fades. These voices of yearning show the spiritual hunger placed by God within every soul. Yet the fullness of what humanity seeks is revealed in the Word who became flesh, Jesus Christ, the light that came into the world to reveal the Father's love and truth.

This book reflects upon that sacred meeting between human search and divine revelation. It recognizes the genuine longing for truth found in India's spiritual heritage while affirming the fulfillment of that longing in Christ, who is the visible image of the invisible God. The aim is not to blend beliefs but to show how ancient questions find their answer in the living Word who entered history to redeem and restore.

The journey of faith begins with wonder and reaches its completion in revelation. The One whom the sages glimpsed as distant is made known personally through Jesus Christ. The Creator whom humanity sought in symbols and silence has spoken in love through His Son. Every ray of truth that touches human hearts points toward the true Light that shines from Calvary.

To walk the path of *Satyam, Shivam, Christam* is to walk toward Him who is the Truth, the Good, and the Anointed One. It is a journey from the human search for meaning to the divine revelation of grace. In Christ, the Eternal Word speaks clearly, offering forgiveness, life, and hope to all who believe.

May every reader of this reflection encounter the wonder of God's revelation, the beauty of His Word, and the transforming power of His Spirit. The Eternal who shaped the universe calls every heart to Himself through the grace of Jesus Christ, the Lord of all truth and the Light of the world.

With faith and hope in His eternal promises,
—**Dr. Venkat Potana.**

Introduction

Every culture carries within it an ancient memory of the Eternal. Humanity has always lifted its heart toward the unseen, asking questions that shape its destiny. What is truth? What is goodness? What lies beyond the visible world? Through ages and civilizations, these questions have never faded. They form the heartbeat of religion, philosophy, and poetry alike.

India, with its vast spiritual heritage, has preserved this longing through sacred hymns, philosophical inquiry, and devotional expression. The Vedas, Upanishads, and the Bhagavad Gita speak of truth as the highest reality and of life as a pilgrimage toward divine understanding. These texts represent humanity's sincere attempt to comprehend the mystery of existence and the presence of the Eternal that governs all. Within their verses shines a profound awareness of divine order, moral responsibility, and the sacredness of life.

The present work emerges from deep respect for that heritage and from a conviction born of biblical revelation. It seeks to engage the reader in a dialogue between humanity's quest and God's self-disclosure. The approach is reflective rather than comparative, invitational rather than argumentative. The author's purpose is to explore how the universal longing for truth and goodness, found in ancient Indian thought, finds its fulfillment in the person and revelation of Jesus Christ.

Satyam, Shivam, and *Christam* together form a triad that expresses this vision. *Satyam* speaks of truth that endures, the foundation upon which all reality rests. *Shivam* points to moral goodness, the beauty of holiness that transforms life. *Christam* reveals the anointed One, the living Word through whom truth and goodness become life-giving realities. The movement of the book follows this sacred rhythm: from the human search for the Eternal to the divine response in Christ who embodies the fullness of what the heart has always desired.

The chapters unfold gradually and intentionally. The first part of the book traces humanity's early awareness of divine order as found in the hymns of the Vedas. It examines the sense of wonder, the moral consciousness, and the intuition of a supreme truth that sustains creation. The second part reflects upon the glimpses of light that appear through moral virtues and ethical ideals within human civilization, showing how these serve as shadows of a greater reality. The third part brings the reader to the heart of revelation where Christ, the eternal Word, enters history and reveals the invisible God in visible form. Later sections of the book interpret selected Hindu scriptures as preparatory reflections that awaken the soul for divine encounter. The final chapters turn from contemplation to application, inviting the reader to live in the light of truth and to embody faith through character and love.

This work stands upon two firm convictions. The first is that divine revelation in Christ is unique and complete, revealing the heart of God with clarity and grace. The second is that the human search for meaning, wherever it appears, reflects the image of God within humanity and therefore deserves both understanding and respect. These convictions form the foundation for a thoughtful dialogue that honors faith while engaging philosophy.

Dr. Venkat Potana writes with both pastoral experience and academic insight. His years of ministry among diverse cultures, along with his study of theology, missiology, and philosophy, have given him a deep awareness of how truth speaks across traditions. His purpose in this book is not to reduce faith to common ideas but to show how the light of Christ illumines every sincere pursuit of wisdom. He invites readers from both Christian and Hindu backgrounds to enter a conversation shaped by reverence, integrity, and openness to truth.

In a world that often separates faith and reason, East and West, spirituality and scholarship, this book offers a bridge of thoughtful engagement. It demonstrates that faith in Christ is neither foreign to India's spiritual soil nor opposed to intellectual inquiry. Rather, it fulfills the ancient longing of the human spirit for a personal, relational encounter with the Creator. Through careful study, scriptural reflection, and contemplative prose, the author seeks to reveal how the Eternal Word unites the quest for truth with the experience of grace.

Satyam Shivam Christam is therefore more than an academic exploration; it is a journey of the mind and heart. It invites scholars to consider the depth of India's metaphysical insight, believers to rediscover the wonder of revelation, and seekers to behold the beauty of divine truth made known in Christ. Each page calls the reader to reflection, gratitude, and awe before the mystery of God's wisdom that transcends culture and time.

As the reader progresses through these pages, the aim is not merely to learn about two traditions but to witness the unfolding of one eternal story: the story of God revealing Himself to humanity and of humanity responding to that revelation with reverence and love. The author's hope is that this book will awaken understanding, inspire dialogue rooted in truth, and strengthen faith in the living Christ who remains the light of the world and the fulfillment of every genuine search for the Eternal.

Part I — The Quest for the Eternal

Every search for God begins with wonder. From the dawn of human thought, the heart has lifted its eyes toward the mystery of existence and sensed a presence greater than itself. Across civilizations and centuries, people have sought to understand the source of life, truth, and beauty. This longing has inspired songs, rituals, and philosophies that reach toward the Eternal who gives meaning to all things.

Part I of this book presents this ancient and universal longing as the foundation of all spiritual pursuit. The human heart does not rest until it encounters the reality from which it came. In these opening chapters, the author traces how early humanity discerned divine presence through nature, conscience, and inner awareness. The seers of India looked upon the heavens, the fire, and the river, perceiving a hidden rhythm that sustains life. They called this order *Ṛta*, the principle of truth that governs the cosmos and guides human conduct. Through this awareness, they understood that moral life and cosmic harmony arise from the same eternal source.

The first chapter unfolds the story of this search for the Eternal through the voice of the Vedas and the meditations of the Upanishads. It reveals how the soul's thirst for truth moves from outward observation to inward realization. The second chapter introduces the mystery of the divine Word, *Vāk*, the creative power through which life and wisdom flow into existence. The third chapter turns to creation itself, showing how every element of the natural world bears witness to the presence of the Creator.

Together, these reflections present a journey of discovery. The human spirit, awakened by wonder, listens to the voice of truth within creation and within the heart. Every movement of thought, every act of goodness, and every spark of devotion arises from this inner call to the Eternal. Through this call, humanity learns that truth is not an abstraction but a living reality, a divine presence that sustains both the world and the soul.

This section prepares the reader to see how divine revelation responds to human seeking. The ancient hymns that spoke of light, fire, and order become the starting point for recognizing the fullness of truth revealed in history. The Quest for the Eternal leads the reader to understand that the same God who placed the desire for truth within the heart also reveals Himself through Word and Spirit. The journey from wonder to revelation, from creation to communion, begins here, guiding the seeker toward the Eternal who is both the source and fulfillment of all truth.

Chapter 1: The Human Heart Seeks the Eternal

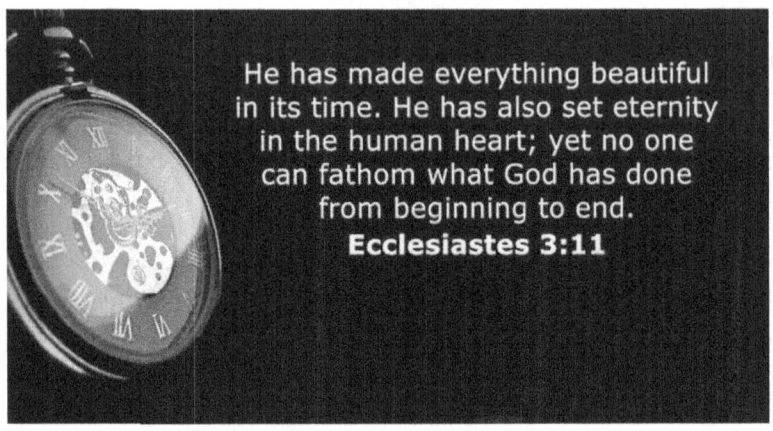

He has made everything beautiful in its time. He has also set eternity in the human heart; yet no one can fathom what God has done from beginning to end.
Ecclesiastes 3:11

1.1 The Universal Search for the Eternal

Every person, at some moment in life, pauses to listen to the quiet questions that rise from the soul:
Who am I?
What is the purpose of my life?
Where did I come from, and where am I going?

These questions are ancient. They have lived in every language and in every age. When the sun sets behind the hills and the earth grows calm, a small voice inside the heart begins to speak. That voice awakens wonder. It reminds the soul that there is something greater than the world of change.

From the earliest times, human beings have looked at the sky, the rivers, and the fire, sensing a power that gives life to all things. The sages of India called this power **Satya** (सत्यम्), meaning truth or reality that does not change. This concept of *Satya* is found throughout the Vedic literature and is often associated with the principle of **Ṛta** (ऋत), the divine order that sustains the universe. The *Ṛg Veda* declares: "O Indra, by truth (*Satya*) the heavens are sustained, by the sun is sustained the earth, by law (*Ṛta*) the region of the mid-air"*(Ṛg Veda 10.190.1–2, Griffith)*.

The poets of the *Ṛg Veda* sang hymns filled with awe. They perceived the order that holds the universe together and called it *Ṛta* — the moral and cosmic rhythm of truth. The sun rises according to

Ṛta, the stars move according to Ṛta, and the human heart finds peace when it walks in harmony with this divine order.

This sense of order is not only seen in the heavens; it also lives within the human conscience. The inner witness that guides a person toward right and wrong reflects *Ṛta* working within the soul. When one acts with kindness, speaks truth, and seeks justice, one aligns with that same eternal rhythm spoken of by the seers.

Across the world, people have heard this same inner call in different ways. The Hebrew psalmist proclaimed, *"The heavens declare the glory of God"* (Psalm 19:1). The Greek thinkers spoke of the *Logos* (Λόγος), the wisdom and reason that orders creation. The seers of India turned inward and discovered the **Ātman** (आत्मन्), the divine Self within, shining quietly behind every breath, as described in the *Chāndogya Upaniṣad*:

"This Self of mine within the heart is smaller than a grain of rice or barley; this Self is greater than the earth, greater than the sky, greater than all these worlds" *(Chāndogya Upaniṣad 3.14.3–4, Müller)*.

Though their languages and symbols were different, their longing was one. Each heart sought to know the source of life, the origin of beauty, the root of love.

This longing does not come from the outside; it rises naturally from within, like a spring hidden beneath the earth. It is a gentle pull toward truth. In the Vedas, this pull is expressed through *Ṛta* — the principle that keeps both the universe and moral life in harmony. Later, the idea of *Dharma* (धर्म) grew from this same root, signifying the right way of living that flows from the eternal order.

Every act of compassion, every search for wisdom, every prayer whispered in the night is part of this movement toward the Eternal. It is as if the universe itself sings a song, and each soul carries a small note of that melody.

Through joy and sorrow, through success and failure, the human heart keeps turning toward the source of that song. Empires rise and fall, generations pass, yet the cry of the heart remains: "Reveal to me the truth that never fades."

Those who have listened deeply have left their words as lamps along the way. Their songs, prayers, and meditations invite us to walk further on this path of light. The journey toward the Eternal has begun, and every step brings a new glimpse of truth.

1.2 The Voice of Wonder in the Vedas

Long before written philosophy or theology appeared, the ancient sages of India, the *ṛṣis* (ऋषि), looked upon the world with hearts full of wonder. They observed the sunrise, the rains, and the rhythm of the seasons. In that harmony, they sensed the presence of something greater, a sacred intelligence that gives order and purpose to all that exists. From that awe were born the hymns of the *Ṛgveda* (ऋग्वेद), among the oldest spiritual songs known to humanity.

These hymns were not written to explain the universe as a theory. They were songs of worship, wonder, and humility. The poets of the Veda did not speak as those who had mastered truth; they spoke as those who had glimpsed it from afar. Their words express reverence, longing, and a heartfelt desire to know the source of life that moves through all creation.

The Hymn of Creation — Nāsadīya Sūkta (नासदीय सूक्त)

One of the most moving hymns of the *Ṛgveda* is the *Nāsadīya Sūkta* (नासदीय सूक्त). The poet begins with words full of awe and honesty: *"Then was neither non-being nor being. There was neither air nor sky beyond. Who knows truly whence this creation came?"*

In these lines, the seer does not claim certainty. He looks at the vastness of creation and stands before it with humility. He recognizes that the universe has a beginning, yet that beginning is shrouded in mystery. The hymn ends with a quiet acknowledgment that perhaps only the Supreme knows the truth, or perhaps even the Supreme alone is hidden in mystery.

This is the voice of sincere seeking. The poet does not argue or define the Eternal; he listens. He gazes upon the stars, feels the pulse of life, and senses a divine presence beyond comprehension. Even today, every soul that stands beneath a silent night sky feels the same awe and wonder.

The hymn invites reflection. In moments of stillness, when the world is quiet, the heart senses a hidden life, breathing love, order, and harmony into existence. It is the first movement of the soul toward the Eternal: wonder.

The Golden Germ – Hiraṇyagarbha Sūkta (हिरण्यगर्भ सूक्त 10.121)

Among the hymns of radiant beauty in the Rigveda stands the *Hiraṇyagarbha Sūkta*, the Hymn of the Golden Germ. The seer sings, "Hiraṇyagarbha arose in the beginning; he was the one Lord of all that is. He established the earth and this heaven. To what god shall we offer our worship?" (Ṛg Veda 10.121.1). These words describe a conscious presence at the origin of creation, a light that gives form and order to all that exists. The poet perceives the universe as arising from this luminous source, the first beginning, the sustainer of life.

The hymn continues, saying, "He who gives breath, he who gives strength, whose command all beings, even the gods, obey; whose shadow is immortality and death, to what god shall we offer our worship?" (Ṛg Veda 10.121.2). Life and order flow from this One, and all beings depend on this sustaining power. The poet recognizes the hidden wisdom and sovereignty behind creation, inspiring awe and reverence. Every movement, every pulse of life reflects a presence beyond comprehension, yet intimately connected to the world.

The seer names this being *Prajāpati*, the Lord of creatures, and *Svarāt*, the self-existent ruler. "He who by his greatness became the one king of the breathing and the sleeping world, who is the Lord of men and cattle, to what god shall we offer our worship?" (Ṛg Veda 10.121.4). In this vision, creation reflects divine intelligence and order. The golden germ symbolizes life that is present even in what seems inert, showing that creation carries a trace of its divine source.

Reading these verses invites reflection on the eternal Word revealed in the Bible. The Word through whom all things were made shines as the eternal source of light, life, and wisdom (John 1:1–4). While the hymn shows an awareness of a divine beginning, the Bible reveals that this beginning is personal, loving, and redemptive, fulfilled in Jesus, through whom all things hold together (Colossians 1:16–17). The golden embryo points toward the reality that the world's life and order are rooted in God's creative will, fulfilled in the eternal Lord Jesus.

The Hiraṇyagarbha Sūkta inspires the heart to seek the Eternal, yet the fullness of that Eternal is revealed in Christ alone. The Rigvedic seer glimpses a source beyond the world, yet the Bible shows the personal God who speaks, redeems, and sustains creation. The golden germ anticipates, in a shadowed way, the revelation of Christ, the true light of the world, the one Lord in whom all life and wisdom are made complete.

The Order Behind All – Ṛta (ऋत)

Throughout the Ṛgveda, the poets speak of Ṛta (ऋत), the divine order that upholds the universe. Ṛta is the rhythm that maintains truth and goodness, the harmony by which the cosmos moves with balance and purpose. The sun rises according to Ṛta, the rivers flow in harmony with Ṛta, and when a person speaks truth or acts with integrity, life aligns with this eternal rhythm. The sages observed that Ṛta governs not only the vast heavens but also the inner landscape of the human heart, guiding conscience, desire, and action. To live in accordance with Ṛta is to live rightly, in harmony with the Eternal presence that sustains all things.

The poets of the Ṛgveda prayed that their minds, words, and deeds might be established in Ṛta. Purity of thought, honesty in speech, and justice in action were seen as living expressions of this divine order. In observing the stars, feeling the pulse of the rivers, and offering worship, the seers recognized a world ordered by truth, in which each action reflects a pattern of life flowing from the Eternal. This awareness of cosmic and moral order awakened a sense of reverence and responsibility, encouraging humans to act with integrity and wisdom.

Ṛta continues to speak to the human spirit today. Every conscience that seeks goodness, every heart that listens to truth, participates in this eternal melody. It is the subtle rhythm that calls the soul to align with the source of life, the hidden harmony that underlies all existence.

In this vision, one sees a reflection of the divine order revealed more fully in the Bible. The psalmist declares that the heavens declare the glory of God (Psalm 19:1), and the Word sustains and upholds all creation (Colossians 1:16–17). Ṛta, glimpsed in the movements of the cosmos and the stirrings of conscience, points toward the ultimate Lord who governs all with wisdom and love. The eternal pattern that the seers sensed in the world finds its fulfillment in Christ, the one in whom truth, life, and order are made complete.

The Flame of Truth – Agni (अग्नि)

Among the most cherished images in the Ṛgveda stands Agni (अग्नि), the sacred fire. The poets of old perceived in fire a visible symbol of the divine presence, a living messenger connecting the human and the unseen. Agni carries offerings from earth to heaven, bridging the worlds and bringing attention to the sacred rhythm of life. The hymn declares, "Agni, you are the light of truth, you are the friend of all who seek" (Ṛg Veda 1.1.1). Fire embodies illumination, warmth, and guidance, revealing what is hidden and sustaining the path of understanding for those who listen.

The flame of Agni carries both outer and inner significance. It burns in the hearth and the ritual altar, yet it also symbolizes the spark within each human heart. This inner fire consumes ignorance, illuminates conscience, and calls the seeker to truth. Lighting a lamp or sacred fire becomes more than a ritual act; it is a remembrance that the Eternal is light, and that every mind and heart can reflect that divine illumination. The fire of Agni mirrors the light of truth present in every soul willing to attend to the call of the Eternal.

The ṛṣis (ऋषि) who composed these hymns stood in awe before creation. Their words do not offer arguments or theories about God; they convey devotion, reverence, and wonder. They describe three movements of the heart: first, amazement at the grandeur of creation; second, recognition of the cosmic order and moral truth; and third, a longing to draw near and unite with the source of that truth. These experiences capture the human impulse to seek, listen, and respond to the Eternal presence.

These hymns continue to guide the seeker today. Every moment of reflection, every attentive heart, resonates with the same movements of wonder, order, and devotion. The light that once inspired the sages of the Ṛgveda (ऋग्वेद) still shines for anyone who approaches the Eternal with openness and humility. The search for truth and alignment with the divine is timeless, present in both the visible world and the quiet depths of the soul.

This vision of fire as the bearer of truth points toward the eternal Light revealed in the Bible. The psalmist declares, "Your word is a lamp to my feet and a light to my path" (Psalm 119:105), and the Gospel shows that Christ is the true light that shines in every heart, bringing life and understanding (John 1:4–9). Agni reflects a shadow of that greater Light, the Eternal Word who sustains and illumines all creation. Through the fire of Agni, one glimpses the deeper truth fulfilled in Christ, the eternal Lord in whom all light, life, and order are complete.

The next reflection will turn inward, exploring the Ātman (आत्मन्), the inner witness of the divine presence, showing how the Eternal speaks within the heart and illuminates the soul from within.

1.3 The Inner Witness (Ātman – आत्मन्)

When a person looks long enough at the world and its beauty, a new discovery begins to arise — the realization that the same mystery that fills the universe also lives within. The sages of India called this inner reality *Ātman* (आत्मन्), the self that is deeper than the body, mind, or emotions.

The *Ātman* is not a separate being that can be seen or measured; it is the very consciousness that makes seeing possible. It is the quiet observer who watches thoughts come and go, the listener who hears the music of life, the one who silently says, "I am." When everything outside changes, this inner presence remains steady, like the still flame of a lamp protected from the wind.

The Upaniṣads, which are the later reflections on the Vedic vision, describe this inner witness with deep reverence. One verse declares:
"The Self is smaller than the smallest and greater than the greatest; it dwells in the heart of every creature."
This idea filled the ancient seekers with awe. They saw that the same power that upholds the stars, the *Ṛta* (ऋत), the eternal order, also guides the human heart from within. The universe and the soul were not separate; both were woven together by the same truth, the same light.

The Hidden Presence in the Heart

The Upaniṣadic teachers often used simple images to describe this truth. They said that within the heart there is a small lotus, and within that lotus there is a shining space where the *Ātman* (आत्मन्) dwells. That space is filled with peace, wisdom, and light. Though the human body may be limited, the presence within is infinite.

The ancient poet of the *Chāndogya Upaniṣad* (छान्दोग्य उपनिषद्) declared:
"This self of mine that lies deep within the heart — smaller than a grain of rice, smaller than a mustard seed — this self is greater than the earth, greater than the sky, greater than all worlds."
In these words, we hear the echo of humanity's timeless longing. The search that began with the stars and the elements turns inward until it finds the divine dwelling in the secret place of the soul.

When one begins to listen to this inner presence, the noise of the world grows quiet. The heart begins to rest. The person who discovers the *Ātman* does not merely find peace; they find purpose. The light that burns within gives direction to life, just as the sun gives direction to the day.

The Witness and the Seeker

The thinkers of ancient India also spoke of the *Sākṣin* (साक्षिन्), the witness within. They said that every thought, emotion, and desire passes before this silent observer. The body may age, the mind may change, but the witness remains untouched. It is pure awareness.

This discovery is profound. It shows that beyond all appearances, there is something eternal within every person. The outer forms belong to time, but the inner witness belongs to eternity. The sages realized that to know this inner presence is to know the source of all existence.

They also understood that not all who look within see clearly. The mind must be purified by truth and humility before the inner light can be known. Just as muddy water cannot reflect the sun, a restless heart cannot perceive the stillness of the *Ātman*. For this reason, the path of inner realization was always joined with the path of righteousness — *Dharma* (धर्म) — the life of truth, compassion, and self-control.

The Breath of Life – Prāṇa (प्राण)

To the Vedic and Upaniṣadic sages, life itself was sacred. They spoke of *Prāṇa* (प्राण) — the life-breath that flows through all beings. They saw that this divine breath sustains every creature, every plant, every moment of existence.

When a person breathes, it is not only air that enters; it is life itself. The rhythm of breathing mirrors the rhythm of the universe. The same presence that gives movement to the stars gives movement to the lungs. In this realization, every breath becomes a silent prayer, every heartbeat a reminder of the unseen giver of life.

The wise teachers said that when the *Ātman* and *Prāṇa* are recognized as one — the inner self and the divine life-breath — a person begins to walk in harmony with the Eternal. Such a person lives with calmness, compassion, and quiet strength.

The Journey Within

When the ancient seekers turned inward, they found that the universe and the soul were not two separate realities but two reflections of one truth. The outer world revealed the glory of the

Eternal through beauty and order; the inner world revealed it through peace and awareness.

This insight brought deep humility. The *ṛṣis* (ऋषि) realized that the highest wisdom does not come from argument or ritual but from silence and surrender. The divine is not reached by climbing upward but by awakening inward.

Every heart that longs for truth still walks this same path. The search for the Eternal always begins outside but must end within. When the soul becomes still and the heart opens, the inner witness begins to speak. That voice does not belong to imagination; it belongs to the Eternal who has always been near.

The discovery of the *Ātman* (आत्मन्) marked a turning point in humanity's spiritual understanding. It revealed that the mystery of God is not far away in the stars but near, closer than our own breath. The same truth that governs the cosmos speaks within the heart.

This realization is not only philosophical; it is deeply personal. The one who knows this presence begins to see life as sacred. Every person becomes precious, every breath holy, every act an offering. The search for the Eternal is no longer a journey through space but a homecoming to the very center of one's being.

From this foundation of inner realization, the path of revelation continues. In time, the Eternal that was sensed in creation and discovered within the heart would take a form that could be seen, touched, and known, the divine entering human history. But that unfolding belongs to the next part of our journey.

1.4 The Hunger for Incarnation: The Divine Draws Near

When the sages looked into the depths of the heart, they found the presence of the Eternal. Yet a new longing began to rise within them. They had known the divine as the unseen spirit, as truth, as order, as light. Now their hearts began to yearn for a closer vision. They desired to meet that Eternal not only as an idea or an inner awareness but as a living presence. This desire gave birth to the ancient hope that the unseen might one day reveal itself in a visible and personal way.

The longing for the divine to draw near is found in many ancient hymns and meditations. The poets prayed that the truth they adored might take form, that the light might shine before their eyes. In every age, humanity has looked for a sign that the Creator is not far away but walks among His creation. This hunger was not born from doubt but from love. It was the desire of a heart that had already tasted the beauty of the Eternal and wished to see it face to face.

The *ṛṣis* (ऋषि) spoke of many expressions of the divine. They sang of *Indra* (इन्द्र), who brings the rain and gives victory to the righteous. They sang of *Varuṇa* (वरुण), who watches over moral law and purity. They called upon *Agni* (अग्नि), the fire that carries offerings to heaven. Yet beneath all these names they sensed one supreme reality that moves through all. The *Upaniṣads* (उपनिषद्) later called it *Brahman* (ब्रह्मन्), the infinite consciousness that is the source of all existence.

Even within these ancient visions, the yearning for a more personal encounter is clear. The poets prayed not only to know the truth but to be touched by it. They asked for the divine to hear, to speak, and to save. The human heart could not rest in abstraction alone. It longed for relationship, for communion, for presence. In every temple, in every offering, there was this silent cry: "Come near, O Eternal One. Dwell among us."

The Desire for the Visible Divine

The Vedic hymns often used the image of light to describe the presence of God. They spoke of *Savitar* (सवितर्), the divine sun, who awakens life each morning. The famous *Gāyatrī Mantra* (गायत्री मन्त्र) prays, "May that divine light illumine our understanding." The longing behind this prayer is not only for wisdom but for vision. The human spirit desires to see the face of truth.

In the *Purusha Sūkta* (पुरुष सूक्त) of the *Ṛgveda* (ऋग्वेद), the seer speaks of the *Puruṣa* (पुरुष), the cosmic person who fills the universe. From His being all things come forth. He is both beyond and within creation. The hymn says, "From Him arose all beings, and He pervades all that is." Here we hear the ancient intuition that the divine is not a distant power but a living reality who can reveal Himself in person.

This vision shows a remarkable truth. The yearning for incarnation did not begin in one culture or one time. It is woven into the fabric of human seeking. Every heart that looks for meaning begins to hope that the unseen truth will take a form that can be known and loved. The *Puruṣa* of the Veda becomes a symbol of that deep hope that one day the infinite will enter the finite, that heaven and earth will meet.

The Cry for Redemption

Along with this longing for nearness, another cry began to rise from the human heart. The sages saw beauty and order in creation, yet they also saw suffering, injustice, and death. They asked why the world that came from truth seems touched by sorrow. They saw that the heart which longs for goodness often fails to do good. The ancient prayer became a plea not only for knowledge but for deliverance.

The poets asked that the divine might cleanse the heart, remove the burden of wrongdoing, and restore harmony. The *Ṛgveda* prays, "May the Lord forgive our hidden faults. May He lead us from darkness to light, from falsehood to truth, from death to immortality." These are not only poetic words. They reveal the deepest human awareness that the Eternal must not only be known but must also act to save. The world needed not only revelation but redemption.

This recognition shaped the spiritual imagination of India. The longing for the one who would come, the one who would restore harmony, became part of its sacred memory. The prayers, sacrifices, and meditations all carried the same expectation that the divine would someday enter the human story with compassion and power.

The Hope of the Ages

Through the centuries, this hope did not fade. It found voice in the *Avatāra* (अवतार) traditions of later texts, which spoke of the descent of the divine into the world to restore righteousness. Each generation believed that when truth declines and falsehood rises, the Eternal reveals Himself to bring back order and peace. Though the understanding of these revelations differed, the longing behind them was the same: that the infinite would draw near and walk among human beings.

The spiritual journey that began with wonder in creation and moved inward to the discovery of the *Ātman* (आत्मन्) now turns outward again in expectation. Humanity waits for the moment when the unseen truth will take visible form, when the light that burns within will shine upon the earth. The heart that has known silence now waits to hear a voice. The soul that has seen the light in meditation now hopes to see the light in history.

The story of humanity's search for God is also the story of God's compassion for humanity. The longing for the divine to draw near was not planted by accident. It is the whisper of the Eternal within every soul, calling creation toward a meeting that was always meant to be.

The hymns of the *Ṛgveda* (ऋग्वेद), the wisdom of the *Upaniṣads* (उपनिषद्), and the prayers of countless seekers together form one continuous melody. They speak of the hunger of the heart that can be satisfied only when the unseen becomes seen, when the eternal truth steps into time.

In that hope, the ancient world waited. The eyes of the seekers looked toward the horizon of time, expecting a dawn when truth would walk among humanity. The next chapter will follow that expectation, as the light that the sages longed for begins to take form in the revelation of the Eternal Word among us.

Conclusion: The Eternal Revealed in Christ

The journey through the human heart's search for the Eternal shows a remarkable pattern. From the earliest awareness of Satya (सत्यम्) and Ṛta (ऋत), through the wonder expressed in the Nāsadīya Sūkta (नासदीय सूक्त) and the luminous presence of Hiraṇyagarbha (हिरण्यगर्भ), to the inner flame of Agni (अग्नि) and the silent witness of the Ātman (आत्मन्), the soul consistently reaches beyond itself, yearning for truth, light, and life that endures. These voices of the sages point to something greater, a reality that orders the universe, sustains conscience, and inspires devotion. Every hymn, every meditation, every act of wonder is a movement toward that source which alone can satisfy the deepest longing of the human heart.

The sages of India glimpsed the mystery; they saw the order, the light, and the breath of life, yet they longed for a presence that could speak, touch, and dwell among humanity. Their words prepare the heart to recognize the One who fulfills the hopes that have always stirred the soul. The longing for order, truth, and redemption finds its ultimate expression in the Word who entered creation, the Eternal who became visible to humanity.

The Bible declares that the Word was with God in the beginning and that all things were made through Him (John 1:1–3). It is in Christ that the eternal truths glimpsed in the Vedic vision are fully revealed. The one who sustains Ṛta, illuminates hearts as Agni, and dwells within as the ultimate Ātman is none other than Jesus Christ, in whom the fullness of light, life, and wisdom is made complete (Colossians 1:16–17). The prayers, the hymns, and the search of every seeker throughout history find their fulfillment in

Him, the Eternal Word who draws near to humanity, meeting the longings of the heart with perfect love and presence.

As we close this chapter, the path that began with wonder and discovery now turns toward recognition and encounter. The Eternal, sought in the stars, the fire, and the self, steps into human history in Christ, bringing the hidden light, the divine order, and the breath of life into tangible, living reality. The heart that has listened to creation and turned inward to its own depths is now invited to behold the Eternal made visible. The journey of seeking continues, but the fulfillment is no longer a distant hope — it is present, embodied, and ever near in Jesus, the one Lord in whom all truth and life converge.

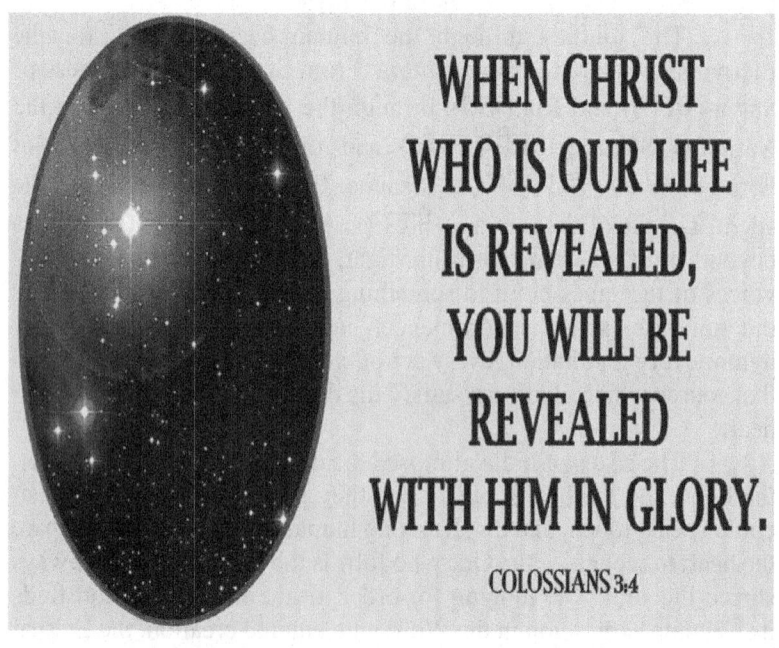

Chapter 2: The Eternal Word in Every Age

2.1. The Mystery of the Divine Word (Vāk – वाक्)

At the dawn of human reflection on the sacred, there is always a voice. Before temples were built, before written scripture captured words on parchment, the Eternal spoke. In the hymns of the Ṛgveda (ऋग्वेद), this divine speech is called Vāk (वाक्), the Word, the source through which the unseen became visible and the unformed became manifest. Vāk is described not as ordinary sound, but as the primal energy that gives rise to all life, the intelligence that orders the cosmos, and the light that illuminates understanding. She is invoked as the mother of all existence, the revealer of truth, and the awakener of creation itself.

The Devī Sūkta (ऋग्वेद 10.125) presents Vāk as a conscious and living presence: "I am the Queen, the gatherer of treasures, the knower of the Supreme. Through me, he who sees, sees; he who breathes, breathes; he who moves, moves" (Ṛg Veda 10.125.1–2, Griffith). Here, Vāk is the source of perception, the power by which life and consciousness are made possible. She is both the mother and the mediator, revealing that all knowledge, speech, and action flow from the Eternal. The hymn emphasizes that creation itself is a manifestation of divine speech, and the cosmos is animated by the Word that orders and sustains all things.

The sages understood that Vāk is eternal and creative. When the divine speaks, reality responds. Like a seed that unfolds into a tree, the Word brings form, structure, and purpose to existence. Every element of life, from the movement of the stars to the breath of the human heart, participates in this divine utterance. There is intentionality in the universe, and every living being is drawn into the harmony of the Eternal Word. In this vision, the world is neither random nor meaningless; it is shaped by conscious speech, animated by wisdom, and suffused with sacred energy.

The Vedic insight into Vāk finds a fuller fulfillment in the revelation of the Bible. The Gospel of John opens with the profound declaration: "In the beginning was the Word, and the Word was with God, and the Word was God. All things were made through Him, and without Him was not anything made that was made" (John 1:1–3). The eternal Word that the Ṛgveda glimpses as Vāk becomes fully personal and redemptive in Jesus Christ. The divine Word is not only the source of creation but the presence who enters history, speaks to humanity, and brings life, light, and understanding. Just as the sages heard the hidden voice that gives form to the universe, every seeker today can recognize the same eternal Word, fully revealed and active in Christ, who upholds all things and calls the human heart to life, truth, and communion with the Eternal.

The Voice Behind All Things

When a person listens carefully to the rhythms of life, to the wind that moves through the trees or the waves that rise and fall, there seems to be a silent melody that connects all things. The Vedic poets sensed this harmony and called it the sound of *Vāk*. It is the song of the Eternal that holds the cosmos together.

They did not think of this Word as a mere sound in the air. They saw it as divine consciousness made audible. Every true word that brings life and truth is an echo of that first voice that spoke creation into being. In this understanding, speech is sacred because it reflects the divine act of communication. The spoken word has power because it mirrors the eternal Word.

This insight gave great dignity to the gift of language. The sages taught that speech should be pure, truthful, and filled with reverence. To speak falsehood was to misuse the gift of *Vāk*. To speak truth was to align the human voice with the voice of the Eternal. Thus, in the ancient world, every hymn, every prayer, every chant was seen as a participation in divine speech.

Vāk and Truth (Satya – सत्य)

In the Vedic vision, *Vāk* and *Satya* (सत्य), the Word and Truth, are one. Truth is not merely correctness of statement but harmony with divine order. The Eternal Word always speaks truth, and through that truth the universe stands firm. When the divine speaks, it does not describe reality; it creates it.

This insight brings deep spiritual meaning. It teaches that truth is creative and alive. Whenever a person speaks truth with love and purity, they join themselves to the very movement of creation. The universe responds to truth because truth belongs to the nature of God. To live truthfully, therefore, is to live in rhythm with the Eternal Word.

The *Bṛhadāraṇyaka Upaniṣad* (बृहदारण्यक उपनिषद्) says that the divine created the world through Word and that every being carries within it the vibration of that first speech. The Word is both the origin and the sustainer of all. Every heartbeat, every breath, every ray of light is a reminder that creation continues to echo the first utterance of *Vāk*.

The Word and the Human Heart

The sages also realized that the divine Word does not only speak in the beginning of time. It continues to speak in the hearts of those who listen. When a person sits in stillness and opens the inner ear, they can sense the same living Word that brought forth the world whispering within them.

This is why the Vedic poets prayed not only to hear *Vāk* with their outer ears but to understand her within. They believed that the human mind and heart were created to receive the divine message. The *ṛṣis* (ऋषि) were called "hearers" because they heard the eternal Word in moments of revelation. Their wisdom was not their invention but their response. They became instruments of *Vāk*, vessels through which the divine spoke to humanity.

This experience made speech sacred. To use words with reverence was to participate in the creative act of the divine. To misuse speech was to disturb the harmony of the world. The same truth applies even today. Words that bless, comfort, and build are reflections of the Eternal Word. Words that wound or deceive move against the rhythm of creation.

The Eternal Word and the Mystery of Being

The mystery of *Vāk* reveals a profound truth about existence itself. All creation is a communication. The universe is not silent; it speaks of its source. Every atom, every living being, every heartbeat carries meaning. The divine Word breathes through all that exists, sustaining it moment by moment.

When the sages realized this, they saw that to live wisely is to listen. To understand life is to hear the voice behind all voices. The Eternal Word is not a sound of the past; it is a living presence that fills the present moment. In every language and in every sincere prayer, there is a reflection of that first speech of love.

The heart that learns to listen to *Vāk* begins to understand that truth and life are inseparable. The divine speaks not only to create but to commune. Every revelation, every inspiration, every act of goodness is a word spoken by the Eternal into the story of the world.

The vision of *Vāk* (वाक्) as the Eternal Word is one of the most beautiful contributions of the Vedic tradition to humanity's understanding of God. It shows that the universe is born of meaning, not of chance. It teaches that speech and truth are holy, that words carry power, and that listening is an act of reverence.

This understanding prepares the heart for a greater revelation. If the Word is the source of all creation and the voice that speaks within, could this Word also reveal itself in a personal way? Could the same truth that spoke the stars into existence one day walk among the very beings it created? The next section begins to explore that question.

2.2 The Word as Revelation

The mystery of the divine Word, *Vāk* (वाक्), shows that creation itself began as an act of speech. Yet the story of the Word does not end with creation. The same voice that spoke the universe into being also speaks to the human heart, guiding it toward truth and goodness. In every age, that Word has continued to reveal wisdom to those who are willing to listen.

The *ṛṣis* (ऋषि) of ancient India did not claim to be the authors of truth. They called themselves "hearers." Their hymns, prayers, and insights were not inventions of the mind but responses to a voice that they heard in the stillness of their souls. They believed that when the heart becomes pure and the mind silent, the Eternal Word can be heard once again. Revelation, for them, was not a sudden idea but a sacred encounter.

This experience gave rise to the *Śruti* (श्रुति), meaning "that which is heard." The scriptures of India were called *Śruti* because they were not composed by human will but received by divine inspiration. The sages listened, and through their listening, divine truth entered human language. The same principle appears in many spiritual traditions of the world, showing that revelation is not confined to one people or one land. Wherever a soul listens with humility, the Eternal Word speaks.

The Living Voice of the Divine

The Word that reveals truth is alive. It is not a message from a distant deity but the living voice of the Creator who continues to speak to creation. When a seeker prays with sincerity, when a poet speaks with purity, when a teacher speaks words that lift the heart toward light, the divine Word is at work.

The *Ṛgveda* (ऋग्वेद) expresses this through beautiful imagery. It says that the Word moves among the gods, among human beings, and among the elements, linking all realms together. It is the bridge between heaven and earth. The Word does not belong to one nation or culture; it belongs to life itself. It is the pulse of the universe and the conscience within every heart.

The Vedic poets described the Word as "hidden in the hearts of the wise." This means that revelation is not forced upon humanity; it is discovered in quietness. The more one turns inward with honesty and humility, the clearer the inner voice becomes. This truth still speaks today, for the Word that revealed itself in the beginning has never fallen silent.

Revelation and Relationship

In every authentic revelation, there is a relationship. The Eternal does not speak merely to inform but to invite. Divine speech is a form of communion. The purpose of the Word is not only to reveal what is true but to draw the listener into a living fellowship with the One who speaks.

The *Upaniṣads* (उपनिषद्) express this relationship beautifully. A student sits before the teacher, filled with reverence, and listens to wisdom that has been passed down from those who first heard the divine Word. The setting is quiet and simple. There are no great rituals, no ceremonies, only the intimacy of truth being shared from one heart to another. Revelation becomes an act of love.

The teacher does not claim ownership of the Word but becomes a servant of it. This humility protects the purity of revelation. When the messenger remembers that truth belongs to the Eternal, not to the human ego, the message remains clear. The moment pride enters, the voice of the Word becomes faint. Thus, revelation and humility are always joined.

The Word as Light

The scriptures often describe revelation as light. Just as light removes darkness and reveals what is hidden, the Word removes ignorance and reveals reality. The *Ṛgveda* (ऋग्वेद) prays, "Lead us from darkness to light, from falsehood to truth, from death to immortality." In this prayer, darkness means confusion and separation from the Eternal. Light means the awareness of divine presence.

When the Word enters the heart, it brings understanding. It does not add new information but awakens the inner knowing that was already planted within the soul. The divine light does not force itself upon a person; it gently illumines the mind until truth becomes self-evident. That is why revelation is often described as awakening rather than instruction.

This experience is the same in every age. Whether in the hymns of the Ṛgveda, in the meditations of the Upaniṣads, or in the psalms and prophecies of other faiths, the Eternal Word speaks to awaken the sleeping heart. Revelation is the sunrise of the soul.

The Continuity of Revelation

The idea that the divine continues to speak is central to the spiritual journey of humanity. The Word that created the world has never withdrawn from it. The same voice that spoke to the ṛṣis (ऋषि) speaks still to those who seek with sincerity.

Throughout history, revelation has taken many forms: a vision in the night, a whisper in the heart, a thought that carries peace, a word of compassion spoken by another person. Every true revelation reflects the same light. The Eternal Word adapts itself to every language, every culture, every time, because truth belongs to all creation.

The sages of India believed that revelation never ends because the Word is eternal. As long as there are hearts willing to listen, the voice of the divine will continue to speak. The journey of faith is therefore not only about reading ancient words but about listening for the living Word that still speaks within and around us.

Revelation is the meeting place between heaven and earth. The divine Word, Vāk (वाक्), speaks through creation, through conscience, and through sacred insight. It does not compel; it invites. It does not demand; it awakens. The purpose of revelation is not to fill the mind with ideas but to fill the heart with presence.

When a person listens with humility and love, the same Word that spoke the stars into being begins to speak within them. This realization gives meaning to every tradition, every scripture, every prayer. The truth that reveals itself is one, though its expressions are many.

In the next section, we will explore how this Eternal Word, which reveals and enlightens, also sustains the universe. The same Word that speaks truth also holds creation together in perfect order.

2.3 The Word as Creation and Order

The eternal Word, Vāk (वाक्), is not only the voice that speaks revelation but also the power that brings the universe into being. In the ancient Vedic vision, every part of creation is the expression of the Word. The sun, the rivers, the mountains, and the wind all exist because the Word gave them life. When the Eternal speaks, being emerges from non-being. This is the mystery of creation through divine speech.

The *Ṛgveda* (ऋग्वेद) describes the Word as the foundation of all order, the principle that sustains everything. It is through the Word that *Ṛta* (ऋत), the eternal cosmic order, is maintained. Every star moves according to this law, every river flows in harmony, and every living being carries within it a reflection of that divine order. The Word is the invisible architect of the universe, the source of rhythm and balance.

The Upaniṣads (उपनिषद्) teach that the Word is not separate from the essence of reality. In the *Chāndogya Upaniṣad* (छान्दोग्य उपनिषद्), it is said that the universe arises from *Vāk* (वाक्) and that all beings are manifestations of this Word. Creation is therefore not random; it is intentional, purposeful, and alive. Every element, every creature, every thought and feeling participates in the unfolding of the divine Word.

The Word as the Source of Harmony

Creation is not only matter and energy but also harmony. The Word that brings forth the universe is also the Word that gives it coherence. Without the Word, existence would fall into chaos. The Vedic sages recognized that the same force that created the stars also guides the human heart. To act in harmony with the Word is to live in alignment with the eternal order.

Ṛta (ऋत) is both cosmic and moral. It governs the rising of the sun and the patterns of human behavior. Every law of nature, every moral principle, is an expression of the Word. When humanity obeys the truth, when hearts act with integrity, they are participating in the same order that holds the galaxies together. The Word, therefore, is not distant. It is active, sustaining life and shaping reality at every level.

The sages saw this order reflected in the rhythms of the world. The seasons, the cycles of birth and growth, the movement of animals and stars, all follow the harmony of the Word. By observing nature, humans could recognize the guiding hand of the Eternal and align themselves with it.

The Word as Sustainer of Life

The Word does not only create; it continues to sustain. Just as the wind keeps the trees swaying, the Word keeps life moving. Every heartbeat, every breath, every thought is maintained by the eternal speech that created existence. Life itself is an ongoing conversation between the Creator and creation.

The Vedic hymns express this beautifully. *Agni* (अग्नि), the sacred fire, is described as carrying offerings to the divine. Through this act, the Word is both honored and continued. Every act of goodness, every truthful word, every act of justice participates in the sustaining of the world. Humanity is called to join the Word, to be a co-creator in harmony with the Eternal.

Even within the heart, the Word continues its work. The inner voice, the conscience, the sense of right and wrong, all reflect the sustaining power of the divine. The Word does not stop at the edges of creation; it flows through the human spirit, guiding and shaping life according to the eternal order.

The Word and Human Participation

The Vedic vision invites every human being to participate in the harmony of the Word. By living truthfully, acting justly, and speaking with integrity, a person aligns with the eternal speech that created the universe. Every moral choice, every act of compassion, every decision to seek truth is a reflection of the Word in human life.

This understanding transforms ordinary life into sacred action. Cooking a meal, planting a seed, helping a friend, or speaking gently to another person becomes an act of participation in divine creation. The Word, once heard only in heaven or in the hearts of sages, now flows through every thoughtful human act.

The sages believed that by following this path, humans could experience unity with the eternal order. The outer world and the inner world, creation and conscience, heaven and earth, all converge through the Word. It is a living reality, dynamic, and present, calling each soul to listen, respond, and live in harmony.

The Word, *Vāk* (वाक्), is the creative principle that sustains all that exists. It is the invisible architect, the source of rhythm, the sustainer of life. It is both cosmic and personal, touching the galaxies above and the human heart below.

By understanding the Word in this way, one can see that creation is not a collection of separate things. It is a living whole, held together by meaning, order, and love. Humanity, as part of this creation, is invited to join in, to participate in the harmony, and to listen to the eternal voice that speaks in everything.

The next section will turn from the Word in creation to the Word in the human heart, showing how the eternal Word continues to guide, inspire, and awaken every soul.

2.4 The Word in the Human Heart

The eternal Word, *Vāk* (वाक्), which spoke the universe into being, continues to speak within every human heart. Long before any written scripture, human beings felt a quiet prompting from within, a presence guiding thought, inspiring action, and whispering truth. The Word enters the heart gently, not as a command but as an invitation to align with eternal reality.

The *ṛṣis* (ऋषि) described hearing the Word as a moment of awakening. In the *Ṛgveda* (ऋग्वेद 10.71.1), the seer Yajñavalkya declares:

"Vāk is the one that brings knowledge; Vāk is the giver of life. She moves among the wise, and through her all beings are sustained."

This verse reveals that the Word is both personal and universal, a reflection of the same eternal Word that shaped the cosmos. It awakens understanding, inspires peace, and illuminates the human mind.

The *Chāndogya Upaniṣad* (छान्दोग्य उपनिषद् 3.14.1) connects the Word with the *Ātman* (आत्मन्), the inner self:

"In the heart of the beings resides the self, the witness, the eternal. By knowing the self, one realizes the Word that pervades all."

The Word and the *Ātman* are intimately connected. Just as *Vāk* sustains creation, it sustains human consciousness. The human heart becomes a place where the eternal Word can dwell, illuminating choices, inspiring love, and awakening the desire for truth.

The Word as Conscience and Guidance

When the Word speaks in the human heart, it often comes as moral awareness, the sense of what is right and good. The sages called this inner voice *Sākṣin* (साक्षिन्), the witness observing every thought and action. This witness guides the seeker toward alignment with *Ṛta* (ऋत), the eternal order.

In *Ṛgveda 10.85.4*, it is written:

"He who knows the Word in his heart, acts with truth, and is righteous in his deeds, lives in harmony with the eternal order."

This reveals that conscience is a reflection of the Word, providing guidance in practical matters. Acts of kindness, honesty, and courage resonate with the eternal order. Every decision to choose truth over falsehood, love over hatred, and generosity over selfishness responds to the Word that speaks from within.

The Word as Inspiration and Wisdom

Beyond moral guidance, the Word inspires creativity, learning, and insight. The Ṛgveda (10.125.5) describes the sages as "hearers" of the Word, saying:

"The wise hear the eternal Word and through it their mind is illuminated with knowledge."

The ṛṣis did not invent the hymns; they received inspiration. Every song, teaching, or meditation was an expression of the Word. This principle continues today: moments of genuine insight, wisdom, or creative inspiration are echoes of the eternal Word. The human mind becomes an instrument to reveal eternal beauty and order.

The inner Word awakens desire, illuminates understanding, and calls the soul to respond. A heart that listens aligns its choices with eternal harmony, gradually reflecting the divine pattern in thought, word, and deed.

The Word as Personal Presence

While the Word sustains creation and inspires the heart, it also becomes deeply personal. The Vedic poets spoke of the divine presence as near to each seeker, guiding, comforting, and sustaining. In Ṛgveda 1.164.39, it is written:

"The Word that moves among the people listens to those who call with a pure heart. She comes near and makes the seeker wise."

The Word is relational. It is not only a force but a companion in life. The heart responds not to abstract principles but to a presence that cares, loves, and draws near. In meditation, prayer, and acts of devotion, the eternal Word communicates directly with the soul, showing that truth is intimately involved in the life of each person.

Through this guidance, the seeker recognizes that the Word is both cosmic and personal, universal and intimately present. This realization forms the bridge between the longing for the unseen and the hope for the Word made visible in history.

The Word, Vāk (वाक्), is alive within the heart. It is conscience, inspiration, and personal presence. It does not compel but invites, does not dictate but awakens. Every sincere heart that listens can hear the eternal Word guiding life toward truth, goodness, and harmony.

Human beings are called not only to observe creation but to respond to the Word within. The inner presence transforms ordinary life into sacred living. Every thought, choice, and action becomes an opportunity to participate in the eternal harmony that sustains the cosmos.

The next section will explore how the Word is recognized across all traditions, showing its universal presence and preparing the heart for the ultimate revelation in history.

2.5 The Universal Vision of the Divine Word

The eternal Word, *Vāk* (वाक्), does not belong to one people or one age. Its presence can be recognized across all traditions, revealing the unity of divine communication throughout human history. From the hymns of the Vedas to the wisdom of the Upaniṣads, and even beyond India, the human soul has always recognized that the cosmos is governed by a living Word, a guiding principle of truth and order.

In the *Ṛgveda* (10.125.1-2), the Word is described as the source of all knowledge and life:

"The Word was in the beginning. Through the Word, all beings came into existence. Those who know the Word know the truth of all things."

This hymn portrays the Word as both the origin of creation and the source of understanding. It emphasizes that to live rightly is to align oneself with the eternal speech that sustains all existence.

The Word in Hindu Tradition

The Upaniṣads (उपनिषद्) expand upon the Vedic vision of *Vāk* as the eternal reality. In the *Mundaka Upaniṣad* (मुण्डक उपनिषद् 1.1.7), it is written:

"By knowing Brahman through the Word, one transcends all ignorance and attains immortality."

Here, the Word is not only a creative principle but also the path to liberation. It is the bridge between the finite human mind and the infinite reality. The Word communicates truth, and the heart that listens can enter into profound understanding.

The *Śvetāśvatara Upaniṣad* (श्वेताश्वतर उपनिषद् 6.9) also speaks of the Word as a personal and living presence:

"He who meditates upon the eternal Word, whom even the gods adore, reaches the highest state of wisdom and peace."

In this way, the Word appears both cosmic and intimate, universal yet personal, guiding the human heart toward the ultimate reality.

The Word in Greek and Jewish Thought

The vision of a universal Word is not limited to India. In Greek philosophy, the concept of *Logos* represents the rational principle that organizes the cosmos. Heraclitus, one of the earliest thinkers to speak of *Logos*, observed that all things are in constant change yet held together by this divine reason. The Word is both order and meaning, similar to the Vedic understanding of *Vāk*.

In Jewish thought, the Word of God (*Dabar*, דבר) carries creation and revelation. In the book of Genesis (1:3), it is written: "And God said, 'Let there be light,' and there was light."

This demonstrates that divine speech creates reality. The Word is active, intentional, and life-giving. It communicates God's presence to the world and calls humanity into relationship with Him.

The Word as a Universal Principle

Across these traditions, the Word performs three essential functions. First, it is the **source of creation**, bringing all things into existence. Second, it is the **sustainer of order**, guiding the universe and human life according to eternal law. Third, it is the **revealer of truth**, communicating divine wisdom to all who listen with sincerity.

The similarities between *Vāk*, *Logos*, and *Dabar* show that the Word is a universal principle, recognized by every culture capable of spiritual awareness. The Word transcends geography, language, and time. It is present wherever truth is sought, wherever goodness is pursued, and wherever the human heart longs for communion with the Eternal.

The Eternal Word speaks to all humanity. Its voice is found in the Vedas, the Upaniṣads, Greek philosophy, and Jewish scripture. This universality prepares the heart for the ultimate revelation of the Word in history.

When the human heart listens, it recognizes the same guiding principle behind every sincere act of truth, wisdom, and love. The Word is not bound by culture or tradition; it moves freely, drawing humanity toward harmony, understanding, and divine presence.

The next section will explore how the eternal Word enters history, revealing itself in a personal, living form, fulfilling the longings that have existed in every heart from the beginning. This prepares the way for the next chapter, which will show the Word made flesh.

Conclusion: The Eternal Word Revealed in History

Chapter 2 has journeyed through the profound vision of the Eternal Word, Vāk (वाक्), tracing its presence in creation, in the human heart, and across all traditions of humanity. From the hymns of the Ṛgveda to the wisdom of the Upaniṣads, from the moral rhythms of Ṛta to the inner witness of conscience, the Word emerges as the living source of life, truth, and order. The sages of India recognized that every sound, every breath, every act of speech participates in this divine utterance. The Word is eternal, creative, and sustaining. It is both cosmic and personal, the invisible force behind the harmony of the universe and the quiet voice guiding each human heart.

Across cultures and ages, this Word has been perceived differently—Vāk in India, Logos in Greek thought, Dabar in Jewish scripture—but its essence remains the same: the Word is life-giving, truth-revealing, and communion-inviting. It is the principle through which all things exist, the order that sustains the cosmos, and the voice that awakens the human soul. Humanity's longing for understanding, for alignment with the divine, and for meaning in existence finds its source in this universal Word.

Yet the Vedic insight, profound as it is, points forward to a fuller revelation. The eternal Word, which created the stars and the human heart, did not remain distant or abstract. In the fullness of time, the Word became flesh in Jesus Christ. The Gospel of John presents this ultimate solution: "And the Word became flesh and dwelt among us, and we have seen His glory, glory as of the only Son from the Father, full of grace and truth" (John 1:14). Here, the eternal Word, which the Ṛṣis and sages glimpsed in creation and conscience, is revealed in history as a personal, living presence. Christ is the Word incarnate, bringing not only creation and truth but redemption, reconciliation, and intimate communion with God.

The biblical solution to the human quest for understanding, moral alignment, and participation in divine order is therefore found in Christ. By listening to His voice, following His guidance, and opening the heart to His presence, humanity enters the harmony of the eternal Word. Creation, conscience, and culture find their purpose and meaning in Him. What was glimpsed in Vāk, Logos, and Dabar is fulfilled in Jesus: the Word who speaks, sustains, and transforms life, inviting every heart into relationship with the Eternal.

In practical terms, this means that living in alignment with the Word involves hearing Christ's voice in daily life, speaking truth in love, acting in integrity, and recognizing the sacred in every encounter. The Eternal Word calls us not only to admiration of the cosmos but to active participation in God's creative and redemptive work. It is in this personal, transformative encounter with Christ, the Word made flesh, that the eternal mysteries of Vāk find their ultimate meaning and fulfillment.

Thus, the chapter closes with a clear invitation: the Word that spoke all creation, that whispers in the human heart, that moves through every culture, now speaks to each of us personally. To heed this Word is to step into the fullness of life, truth, and divine communion. The journey through the eternal Word prepares the soul for the revelation of God's love fully expressed in history, pointing forward to the living Word who walks among us, bringing light where there is darkness, life where there is death, and unity where there is fragmentation.

Chapter 3: The Signs of the Eternal in Creation

From the earliest moments of human awareness, the natural world has spoken to the human heart. Long before temples rose in cities or sacred texts were recorded on palm leaves, people listened to the wind rustling through the trees, the steady flow of rivers, and the dance of sunlight across the mountains. In every culture, there is a recognition that creation is not silent. The hills, the rivers, the skies, and the stars all bear witness to a presence beyond themselves—a presence that invites attentiveness and reflection. In the ancient Vedic tradition, this attentive listening was more than poetic imagination; it was a spiritual practice. The ṛṣis (ऋषि), the seers, observed the cycles of nature, the movement of celestial bodies, and the rhythms of life, discerning the hidden order and intelligence that underlies the cosmos. They called this cosmic order **Ṛta (ऋत)**—the harmony that sustains all things.

To observe creation is to read a text written not in letters, but in forms, patterns, and relationships. Every sunrise, every falling leaf, and every river's meander carries meaning, inviting the mind and heart to recognize the hand of the Eternal. Yet, this recognition requires stillness. It is not enough to glance at the world in passing; one must listen with care. Just as Vāk (वाक्), the Eternal Word, speaks through sound and speech, so too does the divine speak through the language of nature. The world itself is a form of divine communication, a whisper of something greater than what is immediately seen.

Across cultures, humans have sensed this silent conversation. In the forests of India, the rivers were not merely resources—they were living, sacred beings, flowing with the pulse of divine energy. The wind was not only air in motion; it carried messages, a sacred breath of life. Even in distant lands, philosophers and poets have observed a similar pattern: the world is intelligible, ordered, and beautiful, pointing beyond mere chance or material cause. Creation hints at meaning, purpose, and intention. The stars in their courses, the mountains in their steadfastness, the oceans in their rhythm—these are not random phenomena but signs that invite reflection on the presence that sustains and orders all things.

But how does one read these signs? How does the human heart discern the divine within the ordinary, the eternal within the fleeting? This is the question that has guided seekers in every age. The Vedic poets listened with reverence, discovering that the sacred was not confined to temple walls or scripture alone. It flowed in the rivers, blazed in the fire, sparkled in the dew, and sang in the wind. Every element of nature could become a teacher, every pattern a messenger, every moment an opportunity to encounter the Eternal.

As we enter this chapter, we will explore creation as more than a backdrop to human life; it is a living witness to the divine. Light, water, fire, and the very earth itself are carriers of sacred meaning. The cycles of day and night, the rising and setting of the sun, the growth of plants and the flight of birds—all bear the imprint of the Eternal's creative wisdom. Observing creation becomes a form of contemplation, a practice of opening the senses and the heart to the subtle yet profound presence that flows through all that exists.

Yet, this chapter does not seek to declare fulfillment. The Eternal Word, as glimpsed in Vāk, is not yet fully revealed here. Instead, we will gently trace the signs that point toward God's presence, cultivating attentiveness and wonder. In doing so, we prepare the heart to recognize that the world is not a collection of isolated events but a coherent whole, harmonized by a wisdom that invites relationship. Nature, then, is not only a source of beauty and sustenance but also a living testimony to a Creator who is personal, attentive, and intimately involved in every facet of existence.

As we move forward, let us listen carefully to the world around us. Let the rivers speak, let the wind teach, let the sun illuminate, and let the fire reveal. Creation itself, in its rhythm, harmony, and wonder, is a first chapter of divine revelation—a gentle invitation to open the heart and perceive the Eternal at work.

3.1. Nature as the Language of the Divine

Creation speaks, though it has no tongue. The rustling of leaves, the rhythm of rain, the flight of birds, and the stillness of dawn—all form a language that transcends human words. The ancient seers perceived that this world is not mute matter but a living message. The poets of the Ṛgveda (ऋग्वेद) saw in the harmony of the cosmos the utterance of a divine intelligence. They called this harmony **Ṛta (ऋत)**, the eternal order by which all things move in rhythm and truth. In Ṛgveda 1.164.43, the sage declares, *"The one truth (Ṛta) the wise call by many names."* This truth, woven into the fabric of creation, reveals that nature itself is a living text through which the Eternal speaks continually to those who will listen.

The world, then, may be read as a book—an open scripture not written on parchment but inscribed upon the mountains, rivers, and stars. Every sunrise unfolds a page of light; every season turns a chapter in the story of renewal. The forests are lines of poetry in motion, the rivers the flowing sentences of divine thought. This vision is not confined to poetic imagination but reflects the insight that order and beauty point to purpose. The same Ṛta that guides the stars in their courses also shapes the conscience of humankind. When the sun rises unfailingly or the tides return as they always have, the human heart senses a fidelity at work—an echo of the faithfulness of the Eternal.

The Vedic hymns often praise this hidden order through the image of the dawn. In Ṛgveda 1.113.13, the poet exclaims, *"Uṣas shines forth, awakening all life, setting in motion the order of Ṛta."* The dawn does not speak, yet its beauty proclaims faithfulness and renewal. It tells of a universe upheld by a will that delights in light conquering darkness. The river's flow and the rising sun are not accidents of natural law but sacraments of order and grace. They remind the observer that existence is neither chaotic nor meaningless. The universe is intelligible because it is sustained by an intelligent source.

When the ṛṣis (ऋषि) looked upon the natural world, they discerned patterns of interdependence, cycles of death and rebirth, and laws that sustained harmony. They recognized that to live well, one must live in accord with this order. Thus, truthfulness, justice, and reverence for life were not merely moral choices—they were participation in Ṛta itself. In this sense, morality and cosmology were never separate. The physical and the ethical belonged to one seamless reality governed by the same divine law. To act unjustly was to break the harmony of creation; to live truthfully was to dwell within the melody of the Eternal.

In the natural order, the sages saw not only beauty but moral instruction. The seasons taught patience, the rivers taught generosity, the mountains taught steadfastness, and the fire taught purity. The world was a vast school in which every element mirrored a divine attribute. In Ṛgveda 10.190.1–2, it is said, *"Ṛta and Satya (Truth) were born of the blazing heat; from them was born the Night and the flowing Ocean."* Even in creation's earliest hymns, truth and order are not human inventions but divine realities, shaping both cosmos and conscience. The material and the spiritual are intertwined, revealing that to understand creation rightly is to draw near to its Creator.

This vision awakens an enduring intuition: life is purposeful, not accidental. When humans marvel at the symmetry of a snowflake, the rhythm of a heartbeat, or the architecture of a leaf, they glimpse the artistry of the Eternal Mind. Such order does not emerge from chance; it reflects wisdom that designs and sustains. The Vedic poets, standing in awe before the vast sky, did not attempt to master it—they listened. Their wonder became worship, and their worship became knowledge. The sky, the wind, the rain—all were revelations of a Mind that is both immanent and transcendent, near and yet beyond.

The human heart continues to respond to this silent speech. Even today, one who walks beside a river at dusk or gazes upon a starlit sky senses that creation bears meaning beyond its material form. It speaks to something within us that remembers origin and purpose. This recognition does not demand analysis; it invites reverence. In such moments, the heart becomes aware that creation itself is a bridge between the visible and the invisible, between the seen world and the unseen presence that sustains it. The world is not divine in itself but carries the reflection of the Divine—like sunlight dancing upon water, revealing but not becoming the source.

Here, the reflection turns gently toward the deeper revelation that would come in the fullness of time. Just as the Vedic seers discerned the Eternal through Ṛta, so the psalmist would later declare, *"The heavens declare the glory of God, and the firmament shows His handiwork"* (Psalm 19:1). The harmony observed by the ancient poets finds its echo in the biblical vision of a creation that proclaims the Creator. Both recognize that truth and order are not human constructs but divine expressions. Yet the difference lies in direction: the Vedic hymns trace the patterns of the Eternal within creation, while the Bible unveils the personal voice of the Creator who speaks through creation. The former listens to the rhythm; the latter reveals the speaker.

Thus, to read nature rightly is to listen for this voice. The patterns of Ṛta prepare the heart to recognize the faithfulness and wisdom of the One who orders all things. When the believer sees beauty, he gives thanks not to the world itself but to the Eternal who made it. The Vedic seers glimpsed the reflection of that truth in the harmony of creation; the Bible discloses the fullness of that truth in the living Word, through whom all things were made and in whom all things hold together.

In this way, creation becomes not only a mirror but an invitation—to see, to listen, and to love the One whose presence fills all things with meaning. The world is sacred not because it is divine, but because it is the work of the Divine. The rivers still flow by Ṛta; the sun still rises by command; the wind still moves as spirit. All creation continues to speak, and its language is the praise of the Eternal.

3.2. Fire – The Sacred Element

Among all the elements that surround humanity, fire has remained one of the most mysterious and revered. From the first spark that pierced the ancient darkness, fire has been the companion of human civilization—warming the cold, guiding the traveler, transforming the raw into the useful. It is light and heat, comfort and danger, life and judgment. To the ancient mind, this mystery could not be merely physical. Fire seemed alive, breathing and consuming, yet never exhausted. The poets of the Ṛgveda (ऋग्वेद) saw in this living flame a revelation of the Eternal who dwells unseen.

Agni (अग्नि) is celebrated throughout the Vedic hymns as the divine flame kindled both upon the altar and within the heart. In **Ṛgveda 1.1.1**, the poet begins the entire collection of hymns with this invocation: *"I praise Agni, the household priest, the divine minister of sacrifice, who kindles the way to the Eternal."* From the first line of sacred song, fire becomes the symbol of communication between the human and the divine. The flame is the messenger who bears offerings upward and brings blessing downward. It stands at the meeting place of heaven and earth, visible yet pointing to the invisible.

The fire's light reveals what is hidden. It exposes darkness not by violence but by presence. The Vedic sages saw that truth and purity arise through this same principle. When impurity meets flame, it is consumed; when ignorance meets truth, it is dissolved. Thus, Agni is not only the fire upon the altar but the fire within the soul that purifies thought and speech. In **Ṛgveda 3.1.3**, the poet prays, *"Agni, purify us from all deceit and lead us to the path of truth."* The flame becomes both symbol and instrument of inner transformation.

Throughout human history, this sacred perception of fire has endured. The hearth that gathers a family, the lamp that flickers before prayer, the candle that burns at a vigil—all continue the same ancient intuition. Fire awakens awe because it reveals something of divine nature: it gives light, yet it consumes; it warms, yet it refines. To sit before a flame is to sense that life itself is a burning mystery—constantly perishing and renewing, never static, always alive. In this mystery the heart begins to understand why the Eternal is often compared to fire. The prophets of the Bible spoke in the same language of revelation. Moses encountered the Divine Presence in a bush that burned yet was not consumed (Exodus 3:2). Later, the psalmist would sing, *"The Lord wraps Himself in light as with a garment"* (Psalm 104:2). What the Vedic seer intuited as the purifying flame, the Bible reveals as the living presence of the Eternal who is light and in whom there is no darkness at all.

Thus, the sacred fire points beyond itself. It is not an object of worship but a sign that draws the soul toward the One whose truth enlightens and whose love refines. Every spark, every flame, every light that shines in the night becomes a quiet reminder that the Eternal still speaks through creation. The same fire that warmed the hands of the ancient sages now burns within every seeking heart, calling each soul to draw near to the light that never fades.

3.3. Rivers and Water – Life and Flow

From the beginning of time, rivers have been the lifelines of the earth. They carry the music of creation across valleys and plains, giving drink to the thirsty, fertility to the soil, and refreshment to every living thing. Flowing with unceasing rhythm, the rivers speak of movement, renewal, and generosity. Every drop bears a story of life shared freely. To the heart that watches their current, rivers whisper of the Eternal, whose presence sustains and renews all things.

The sages of ancient India saw in water the very breath of existence. In **Ṛgveda 10.9.1**, the poet prays, *"Waters, you are the ones who bring health and joy; may you sustain us, that we may see great delight."* These words show deep reverence for the element that nourishes body and spirit alike. The rivers were not only physical streams but sacred presences, symbols of divine compassion and abundance. The hymns speak of Sarasvatī, the river that enlightens, and of Gaṅgā (गङ्गा), whose waters are regarded as purifying and life-giving. To bathe in the river was to touch the living current of the Eternal that flows through creation.

Water has always been more than a physical necessity; it is the mirror of the soul. When still, it reflects the sky; when stirred, it moves with irresistible force. The Ṛgvedic poets understood this mystery. In **Ṛgveda 7.47.2**, the seer prays, *"May the waters bring us refreshment, may they gladden our hearts and cleanse us from every wrong."* Such verses reveal how the outer cleansing of water expresses the inner longing for purity. The rivers teach that life must keep flowing; stagnation leads to decay, but movement renews and heals.

As one stands beside a river, the steady current seems to speak a gentle truth. Life, like the river, must continue its course, receiving and giving, washing away what is old, and making room for what is new. The one who listens deeply can hear, within the murmur of the stream, the same voice that called creation into being. Just as the waters carry light from the mountains to the sea, so the spirit of the Eternal flows through time and heart alike.

In the Bible, this mystery finds its full echo. The psalmist sings, *"There is a river whose streams make glad the city of God"* (Psalm 46:4). The prophet Isaiah speaks of the Eternal who says, *"I will pour water on the thirsty land and streams on the dry ground"* (Isaiah 44:3). Finally, in the words of Jesus, the image reaches its fulfillment: *"Whoever believes in me, out of his heart shall flow rivers of living water"* (John 7:38). The rivers of the earth thus become signs of a deeper reality, pointing to the life that flows from the Eternal and renews the soul.

Each spring, each stream, and each drop reminds humanity that life is a sacred gift. As the rivers never cease to move, the heart that remains open to the Eternal will never run dry. The flow of water becomes the song of divine mercy, calling every being to live, to forgive, and to begin again.

3.4. Light – Illumination and Presence

Light has always been one of humanity's purest experiences of the Eternal. When the first rays of dawn touch the horizon, a quiet transformation begins. The darkness retreats, colors awaken, and life rises again to meet the day. The same sun that shines upon the mountains of India warms the deserts, seas, and fields of every land. Its radiance speaks in silence, revealing the order and goodness that sustain all living things. To every human heart, light brings assurance, guidance, and hope.

The seers of the Ṛgveda (ऋग्वेद) looked upon the sun, Sūrya (सूर्य), as the visible form of divine truth. In **Ṛgveda 1.50.10**, the poet prays, *"Behold the radiance of the god who rises, who moves by his own might. May we approach that light of Sūrya, the most splendid* *of all lights."* The verse captures a universal moment of reverence. The sun is not worshiped as a mere object in the sky but honored as the expression of the hidden power that gives warmth, order, and life. It is through this light that the world is seen, and through its rising that the heart learns to hope again.

Light in the Vedic vision is not only physical brightness. It is the symbol of awakening, knowledge, and truth. The Upaniṣadic teachers later echoed this in their prayer, *"Lead me from darkness to light, from the unreal to the real, from death to immortality"* (Bṛhadāraṇyaka Upaniṣad 1.3.28). The longing expressed in this verse is timeless. Every human being feels the desire to move from confusion to clarity, from fear to peace, from ignorance to understanding. The shining of light upon the mind mirrors the enlightenment of the soul.

When a person sits quietly beneath a starlit sky or watches the moon rise over a river, something in the heart becomes still. The lights of heaven remind us that the universe is filled with order and meaning. The stars follow their courses without haste or rest, the moon governs the tides, and the sun marks the rhythm of time. These patterns are signs of the Eternal's faithfulness, teaching humanity that the same power which governs the heavens also guides the path within. The light outside becomes a parable of the light inside, the illumination of conscience and spirit.

In the Bible, light carries the same majesty and tenderness. The psalmist declares, *"The Lord is my light and my salvation"* (Psalm 27:1). The prophet Isaiah proclaims, *"The people who walked in darkness have seen a great light"* (Isaiah 9:2). And the Gospel reveals the Eternal Word as the true source of all illumination: *"In Him was life, and the life was the light of men. The light shines in the darkness, and the darkness has not overcome it"* (John 1:4–5). The radiance that the Ṛgvedic poet saw in Sūrya finds its ultimate fulfillment in the divine light revealed through the Word, whose presence enlightens every heart.

When dawn breaks after a long night, the first glow of morning always brings peace. In the same way, the light of the Eternal awakens the inner world, dispelling fear and revealing truth. Those who open their hearts to that light find that it does not fade with the setting sun. It lives within, guiding thought, purifying motive, and revealing the path that leads to life. The sun, the moon, and the stars thus become reflections of a deeper radiance—the light of the Eternal, shining forever in creation and in the soul.

3.5. The Rhythm and Harmony of Creation

When one looks closely at the world, a pattern of rhythm and harmony emerges in every direction. The earth turns, the seasons change, the tides rise and fall, life is born and passes away — yet all unfolds in a mysterious order. The morning follows night, the seed hidden in the soil bursts forth in spring, and even decay gives way to renewal. Beneath the vast complexity of creation lies a quiet constancy, a pulse that keeps the universe alive. This harmony is not mechanical; it is musical — a sacred rhythm through which the Eternal sustains all things.

The ancient seers of the Ṛgveda (ऋग्वेद) recognized this underlying order and called it **Ṛta (ऋत)** — the principle of truth, harmony, and rightness that governs both nature and moral life. Ṛta is the reason why rivers flow within their banks, why stars hold their paths, and why truth is stronger than falsehood. In **Ṛgveda 10.190.1–2**, it is said: *"From Ṛta arose the shining light; from Ṛta the night and the day are born. Ṛta sustains the sun in the heavens."* The verse reveals that the stability of the cosmos rests upon a divine foundation. The world is not ruled by chance but by truth, and that truth is rhythmic, living, and good.

This awareness gave birth to profound reverence. The Vedic poets saw that the same order governing the stars also governs the human heart. When one speaks truth, acts with justice, and lives in harmony, one aligns with Ṛta — participating in the same rhythm that holds the heavens in place. Injustice, deceit, and disorder were seen not merely as moral failings but as disturbances in the fabric of creation itself. Thus, to live rightly was to live in tune with the cosmic song.

Even what appears to be chaos bears traces of rhythm. Storms arise, fires consume, and lives end — yet from these movements comes renewal and balance. The seed must break before it grows; the forest must burn before new life springs forth. Nature's harmony includes both stillness and motion, birth and death, calm and storm. The apparent disorder is itself contained within a greater order, a sign that the Eternal's wisdom pervades even the places we call wild.

This insight finds deep resonance in the Bible. The psalmist sings, *"The heavens declare the glory of God; the skies proclaim the work of His hands. Day after day they pour forth speech"* (Psalm 19:1–2). The prophets, too, saw creation as ordered by divine faithfulness: *"As long as the earth endures, seedtime and harvest, cold and heat, summer and winter, day and night shall not cease"* (Genesis 8:22). What the Vedic sages intuited through Ṛta — that there is an intelligent order binding heaven and earth — is affirmed in the biblical revelation of the Creator who sustains all things by His Word.

To live attentively within this order is to participate in divine wisdom. The cycles of nature teach humility and gratitude; they remind humanity that existence is neither accidental nor self-sustained. The same harmony that turns the galaxies also shapes the human heart, inviting every soul to walk in step with truth. Creation, then, is not merely scenery — it is a living rhythm of grace, a continual reminder that the Eternal speaks not only through words but through the music of being itself.

3.6. Creation as a Mirror of the Human Heart

When the ancients gazed upon the world, they did not see a lifeless landscape. They saw reflections of themselves — the rhythms of their own breath in the wind, the pulse of their hearts in the beating of rain, the flicker of their thoughts in the shimmer of flame. Nature was not separate from the human spirit; it was a mirror. The outer world revealed something of the inner life, and the patterns of creation whispered the mystery of what it means to be alive.

The Vedic sages often spoke of this deep correspondence between the universe and the human being. The macrocosm — the vast, ordered cosmos — finds its echo in the microcosm of the individual soul. In **Ṛgveda 10.90 (Puruṣa Sūkta)**, the universe itself is portrayed as the body of the Eternal Person, from whose being all creatures and all elements arise. Humanity, in this vision, carries within itself the structure of the cosmos: breath mirrors the wind (*vāyu*), thought reflects the sun (*sūrya*), and inner fire (*agni*) burns as consciousness. To know oneself is, therefore, to glimpse the order and unity that holds the universe together.

This vision finds a striking resonance in the Bible's understanding of humanity as created "in the image of God" (Genesis 1:27). The human being is not an isolated creature but a reflection — a living image of the Eternal's wisdom, love, and creativity. Just as the heavens declare His glory, the human heart bears witness to His likeness. When the psalmist prays, *"You formed my inward parts; You knit me together in my mother's womb"* (Psalm 139:13), he speaks of this same intimacy between Creator and creation. The human person is not merely within the world; the world, in some mysterious way, is also within the person — carried in thought, memory, and longing.

Every element of creation invites inward reflection. The calm of dawn mirrors the peace of a quiet mind; the storm reflects the turbulence of emotion; the rhythm of seasons parallels the soul's journey through loss and renewal. To perceive these patterns is not to romanticize nature but to recognize that the Eternal has woven a single thread through both the seen and the unseen. The order that shapes the stars also shapes the conscience; the beauty of the world calls the heart to harmony with its Maker.

In the act of contemplation, the human being stands between heaven and earth — capable of perceiving both the grandeur of the cosmos and the depth of inner life. When one listens deeply, creation becomes not a distant spectacle but a conversation. The whisper of wind through the trees, the reflection of light on water, the silence between breaths — all become signs of divine nearness. Through the mirror of creation, the heart discovers its own longing for the Eternal, and in that longing, it finds the path home.

3.7. The Presence of God in Gentle Ways

There are moments in life when the Eternal does not speak through thunder or fire but through quietness — in the rhythm of a bird's song, the softness of rain, or the calm glow of evening light. The world, when truly observed, becomes a sanctuary of gentle communication. In such moments, the presence of God is not distant or abstract but near, almost tender, woven into the smallest details of life.

The ancient poets of the **Ṛgveda (ऋग्वेद)** recognized this gentle nearness. They sang of the Eternal as one who "upholds both earth and sky" and who "moves among creation unseen yet sustaining all" (Ṛgveda 10.121). To them, divinity was not confined to temple or altar but diffused throughout existence — in wind, in fire, in breath, in the beating of the heart. The world itself was a living testimony of divine care. Every sunrise was a renewal of promise; every drop of rain a sign of mercy. The poets perceived that behind the harmony of nature stood not a cold order but a benevolent will — one that nourished life and invited gratitude.

This vision finds a quiet correspondence in the biblical witness. When the psalmist declares, *"The earth is full of the goodness of the Lord"* (Psalm 33:5), he too affirms that divine care is not occasional but constant. The Eternal does not merely create and withdraw; He sustains and provides. The grass that grows in silence, the stars that shine in their appointed places, and the breath that fills every living creature all bear the imprint of His goodness. The prophet Elijah discovered this truth when he encountered not a storm or an earthquake but "a still small voice" (1 Kings 19:12). The Eternal reveals Himself not only in might but also in tenderness.

The gentle presence of God is often felt rather than seen. It stirs in moments of awe and gratitude, in the wonder that arises when one beholds beauty that seems too perfect to be accidental. A flower unfolding in the wilderness, a mother's care for her child, the quiet resilience of a tree in winter — all reflect the same mysterious compassion that sustains the universe. Such experiences do not demand explanation; they invite reverence.

In both the Vedic and biblical visions, creation is not an indifferent mechanism but a living dialogue between the Creator and the created. The Eternal speaks in ways that nourish rather than overwhelm, inviting hearts to listen rather than fear. To those who pause and attend, the world becomes a living parable — its beauty a reflection of divine generosity, its harmony a sign of divine wisdom, its fragility a reminder of divine patience.

To live with this awareness is to walk gently through the world, recognizing each moment as a gift. Awe turns into gratitude, and gratitude deepens into worship. The same Eternal who kindled the sun's fire and set the rivers in motion continues to whisper through creation today — calling the heart not to escape the world, but to see in it the traces of His loving presence.

3.8. Lessons from Creation

Creation is not only a scene of beauty but a teacher of wisdom. Those who learn to listen to its quiet lessons discover that every living thing carries a message of the Eternal. The rhythm of the seasons speaks of patience; the steady course of the rivers teaches perseverance; the growth of a seed into a tree reveals hidden purpose and faithfulness. The world instructs not through argument, but through example — silently shaping hearts to live in reverence and humility.

The sages of the **Ṛgveda (ऋग्वेद)** understood this truth deeply. They observed that when humanity walks in harmony with the cosmic order, life flourishes. To violate that order is to lose peace within and without. Thus, they prayed, *"May we walk in Ṛta, may our hearts be established in truth, may our speech and deeds accord with the law of the Eternal"* (Ṛgveda 1.164). This prayer was not merely ritual; it was ethical. The poets perceived that the same harmony guiding the stars also calls humanity to live justly, to honor life, and to care for the earth as sacred trust.

Such wisdom finds a natural echo in the biblical vision of stewardship. In the opening pages of the Bible, humanity is placed within creation not as its owner but as its caretaker, called to "tend and keep" the garden (Genesis 2:15). The created world is not a possession to exploit but a gift to nurture. Every act of reverence toward nature becomes, in this light, an act of worship toward the Giver of life. The humility of the farmer, the patience of the gardener, and the mindfulness of the pilgrim walking under the open sky all mirror the heart that honors the Creator by honoring His creation.

To observe creation rightly is to grow in virtue. Its silence teaches listening; its cycles teach trust; its vastness teaches awe. Mountains and rivers do not rush, yet they accomplish their purpose. The sun never forgets to rise; the stars keep their appointed paths. Such constancy inspires the soul to live with faithfulness, and such harmony reminds humanity of its place within the greater design of the Eternal.

When the eyes of the heart open to see divine wisdom reflected in the natural world, they are also prepared for a deeper revelation. The patterns of order, beauty, and compassion seen in creation find their fullest meaning in the revelation of God's heart through the Word made flesh. Just as creation reveals the mind of the Eternal, so the coming of the Eternal into creation reveals His love. Every sunrise that speaks of renewal, every seed that dies to bring forth life, quietly prefigures this greater truth — that the Creator who shaped the world with wisdom also seeks to renew it with grace.

Thus, the lessons of creation are not distant or abstract; they are invitations. They call every heart to stewardship, gratitude, and worship — to walk in harmony with the Eternal order and to recognize, in the beauty of the world, the gentle traces of the One who made it.

3.9. Creation as Universal Language

Long before nations, creeds, or sacred books, creation itself spoke. The sun that rises upon every land, the wind that breathes through every valley, and the stars that shine over every people form a universal language that no tongue can divide. The cosmos is a text written not in letters but in light — a revelation open to all who have eyes to see and hearts to understand.

The sages of the Ṛgveda (ऋग्वेद) listened to this language and discerned the harmony of Ṛta, the divine order that holds all things together. In their hymns, they perceived that truth and goodness are not inventions of culture but reflections of a higher law woven into the fabric of existence. This insight finds a quiet correspondence in the words of the Bible: "The heavens declare the glory of God, and the sky proclaims the work of His hands" (Psalm 19:1). Both the Vedic seer and the Hebrew psalmist gazed upon creation and heard a voice beyond sound — the Eternal Word speaking through the rhythm of life itself.

Across centuries and civilizations, this universal witness has stirred the same human response: awe before the vastness of being, wonder at the mystery of order and beauty, and a moral intuition that goodness is real and meant to be lived. Such awareness prepares the soul for revelation. It teaches that the One who shaped the stars also speaks within the conscience, guiding every heart that seeks truth.

In fact, creation becomes the first meeting place between God and humanity. Its language is older than scripture and wider than speech. It unites all seekers in a common awareness of the Eternal. Yet this language also invites a deeper hearing — for the Word that once echoed through the cosmos will soon speak within history itself, revealing the heart of the Eternal in a more personal and redeeming way.

Conclusion: The Whisper of the Eternal

Creation stands as both mirror and messenger. Every mountain that lifts its silent peak, every river that sings as it moves toward the sea, every flame that burns with living light speaks of a Presence greater than itself. The world is not a random gathering of matter but a living testimony — a continuous hymn of order, beauty, and meaning. To see rightly is to listen with the heart, for creation does not shout; it whispers.

Through its rhythms and harmonies, the Eternal invites rather than compels. The seasons come and go with patient grace; the stars remain steadfast in their appointed places; the earth nourishes without demand. In all these gentle movements, we glimpse a God who is relational, not coercive — a presence that draws rather than drives, that offers love rather than control.

For those who have eyes to see and ears to hear, creation becomes a sacred conversation. It teaches humility when we behold its vastness, gratitude when we receive its gifts, and awe when we sense its mystery. The same hand that shaped the stars shapes the heart, and the same light that dawns in the sky seeks to rise within the soul.

And so the journey continues. The world around us has spoken; now the Eternal begins to speak more personally within. The voice that whispered through the river, the fire, and the wind will soon be heard in the stillness of the human spirit. The question that remains is simple yet profound:

Where do you notice the whisper of the Eternal in your own life? What lessons does creation teach your heart?

Part II — The Glimmers of Truth

Every soul carries within it a light that points toward the Eternal. Though the fullness of divine revelation shines perfectly in Christ, traces of that light have touched every civilization and culture through conscience, wisdom, and moral awareness. Humanity, created in the image of God, has always possessed the capacity to perceive goodness and truth, even amid the limitations of its understanding. These reflections of divine light may appear as glimmers, yet they awaken the heart to seek the One from whom all truth flows.

Part II of this book explores these sacred reflections as they appear within human experience and within the moral vision of Hindu tradition. The sages of India perceived that the order governing the universe also shapes the moral life of humanity. They taught that to live truthfully, to act with righteousness, and to honor all life is to live in harmony with the divine order. These insights reveal that the moral law written upon the human heart is a silent witness of the Creator's nature and will.

The chapters that follow explore the values that have guided the human conscience through ages. *Dharma* expresses the principle of right living, calling humanity to walk in balance and integrity.

Satya reflects the power of truth that sustains every relationship and holds the universe together. *Ahimsa* affirms the sacredness of life and the virtue of compassion that arises from recognizing divine presence in all creation. These and other moral insights form the ethical framework through which humanity learns to discern the difference between good and evil, light and darkness, harmony and disorder.

The author approaches these themes with deep reverence, recognizing that they represent humanity's sincere response to divine prompting. Each virtue described in the Vedic and post-Vedic traditions stands as a mirror that reflects aspects of divine character. Through the practice of truthfulness, purity, humility, and self-control, the human heart becomes more sensitive to the presence of God. These glimpses of moral beauty serve as preparation for the greater revelation of grace and redemption revealed in Jesus Christ, who embodies truth and love in perfect unity.

Part II, therefore, reveals that the moral awareness found in ancient cultures is not a human invention but a divine gift. The light of conscience, the sense of justice, and the desire for righteousness all come from the same Eternal source who sustains creation. As readers move through this section, they are invited to see how these glimmers of truth point toward the fullness of light that shines in Christ. Through this understanding, the moral intuitions of humanity are seen not as separate paths but as signposts guiding the heart toward the One who is Truth itself, the Eternal Word who enlightens every person that comes into the world.

Chapter 4 Shadows of the Eternal

From the earliest stirrings of consciousness, the human heart carries a subtle, persistent longing. It reaches beyond the surface of daily life, sensing that there is more than mere survival or comfort. Even in moments of beauty—a quiet morning, a gentle breeze, the laughter of a child—there emerges a silent question: Is there a source from which all goodness and harmony flow? This yearning is not confined to one culture or era; it is a universal pulse within humanity, a recognition that life contains dimensions of truth, moral order, and beauty that exceed what we can create for ourselves.

In the spiritual texts of ancient India, this longing is reflected in the moral and ethical ideals that guide human living. Dharma, satya, and ahimsa are not only practical principles; they are subtle reflections of a higher reality, hints of a perfection that surpasses human effort. Observing the patterns of duty, truthfulness, and reverence for life awakens the awareness that the human heart is made for something greater. Even when these ideals are partially realized or imperfectly lived, they point to a moral horizon that calls the seeker beyond themselves.

As we begin to explore these shadows of the Eternal, we can ask ourselves: How do moral and ethical life reveal glimpses of the divine? How does the pursuit of goodness and truth stir within us a sense of incompleteness that longs for fulfillment? In Hindu scripture, these questions find expression not in abstract arguments but in lived experience—through observation of right action, cultivation of virtue, and reflection on the heart's subtle stirrings.

This chapter invites the reader to notice the shadows themselves, not yet the full light. It asks us to observe how the pursuit of moral integrity, the practice of truthfulness, and the reverence for life act as signposts toward a reality beyond immediate perception. In doing so, the heart begins to recognize its natural orientation toward the fullness of God. The experiences of longing, awe, and ethical striving are not isolated human phenomena; they are invitations to perceive the presence of the Eternal gently working through conscience, intuition, and moral aspiration.

Thus, the human heart is prepared to see that even incomplete understanding or imperfect moral practice carries significance. These "shadows" of divine order guide us toward anticipation, inviting us to turn inward with attentiveness, outward with compassion, and upward with hope. In recognizing the partial glimpses of goodness, truth, and reverence, the heart begins a journey toward the fullness that lies beyond itself, ready to encounter the personal, relational God who fulfills every longing and illuminates every moral ideal.

In fact, the human experience of moral aspiration and ethical striving becomes a language of the heart, a silent dialogue with the Eternal, preparing us to understand that shadows themselves are signs pointing toward the source of all life, truth, and beauty.

4.1 Dharma – The Path of Righteous Living

In the Vedic worldview, dharma signifies more than mere rules or social obligation. It is the guiding principle of righteous living, a pattern of moral order that connects human action with the cosmos itself. The Rig Veda emphasizes the importance of right conduct in maintaining harmony, stating, "Through truth and righteousness, the worlds are upheld" (Rig Veda 10.191.2). Dharma is therefore both personal and communal, encompassing duty, ethical responsibility, and alignment with Ṛta, the cosmic order that sustains all life.

Living according to dharma cultivates inner harmony. It calls the individual to act with integrity, courage, patience, and compassion. The Bṛhadāraṇyaka Upaniṣad observes that a person who follows dharma aligns with the eternal order, noting, "By truth and good conduct, one attains the highest goal" (Bṛhadāraṇyaka Upaniṣad 4.4.5). Ethical living, then, is not a set of external rules but a resonance of the heart with the moral fabric of the universe. Even when actions are challenging or misunderstood, adherence to dharma nurtures a sense of inner coherence and clarity.

On a societal level, dharma strengthens the bonds between people. When individuals act with fairness, honesty, and care, communities thrive and justice is realized. Manu's Dharmashastra states, "By observing righteousness, the world remains in order" (Manu 4.138). Dharma thus functions as a stabilizing force, weaving human actions into a larger tapestry that reflects cosmic harmony. Moral effort in daily life, whether in interpersonal relationships, work, or civic responsibility, manifests the principles of dharma concretely and visibly.

Yet dharma is never a claim of perfection. Humans are prone to error, and circumstances often test moral resolve. Even so, every effort to choose truth over falsehood, generosity over selfishness, or patience over impatience reflects a participation in a moral reality that transcends the individual. The Mahābhārata echoes this insight: "By striving in righteousness, one moves closer to the divine, even when mistakes are made" (Mahābhārata, Shanti Parva 133.34). Ethical action becomes a way of glimpsing the Eternal, as the heart that seeks virtue senses the presence of a higher moral source.

The lived experience of dharma awakens moral awareness and spiritual sensitivity. Moments of decision, when conscience asserts itself, or when courage is required in the face of fear, reveal that ethical life is relational. The heart that acts rightly begins to perceive a moral universe that is coherent, intentional, and good. Dharma transforms ordinary life into an arena of spiritual discovery, where human choices resonate with a larger order that is beyond comprehension yet deeply perceptible.

Dharma can be understood as a shadow of the Eternal, a reflection of the divine order that shapes both the cosmos and the human heart. Every ethical decision and act of moral courage participates in this order, inviting humans to align with the source of truth, goodness, and wisdom. As the Rig Veda declares, "Righteousness and truth bring prosperity to the seeker who follows the path" (Rig Veda 1.33.12). Dharma is the initial glimpse of the Eternal in human experience, preparing the soul to recognize the fullness of God beyond the shadows of moral striving.

By observing and living according to dharma, the human heart begins to attune itself to the rhythm of divine order, discovering that ethical life is not merely social necessity but a participation in the harmony and wisdom of the Eternal.

4.2 Satya – Truth as Guiding Light

In the Vedic tradition, satya is far more than mere factual correctness. It is the alignment of speech, thought, and action with ultimate reality, the principle that sustains the cosmos and gives coherence to human life. The Rig Veda declares, "Truth is the foundation of all existence; by it the worlds are upheld" (Rig Veda 10.65.6). Truth is inseparable from moral order and spiritual insight, reflecting a reality that is both eternal and alive.

Satya manifests in human experience when words and deeds resonate with integrity. Speaking truth, acting honestly, and perceiving reality without distortion are not only social necessities but expressions of a cosmic principle. The Atharva Veda observes, "One who follows truth walks in the path of light and reaches the immortal" (Atharva Veda 19.53.1). Truth has the power to illuminate the mind, awaken conscience, and draw the seeker into harmony with the eternal order.

Human conscience has an intuitive response to truth. Even when circumstances complicate moral choices, there is a natural recognition of what is right. The Bṛhadāraṇyaka Upaniṣad states, "By knowing the eternal, one knows what is right and what is false; the heart discerns the order of the worlds" (Bṛhadāraṇyaka Upaniṣad 2.1.17). This response suggests the presence of a transcendent moral anchor, a source beyond human invention that calls each person to integrity and awareness.

The power of truth is transformative. Satya shapes character, refines judgment, and fosters trust and harmony among people. The Mahābhārata teaches, "Truth protects those who are steadfast in it, even in the midst of adversity" (Mahābhārata, Shanti Parva 243.9). In this way, truth functions as a guiding light, not only revealing reality but also orienting the human heart toward moral clarity and spiritual growth.

Truth points beyond itself to a higher source. Every act of honesty, every sincere word, and every faithful adherence to what is right carries a reflection of the Eternal. Even when unacknowledged, truth leaves a trace of divine order in the world. The Vedic seers recognized that ethical life guided by truth is a pathway toward experiencing a greater reality, a reality that fulfills the human heart's yearning for justice, harmony, and purpose.

Awareness of satya also cultivates discernment. By observing the effects of truth and falsehood in personal life and society, humans learn to perceive patterns that suggest intentionality in the moral universe. Life aligned with truth resonates with peace, consistency, and a sense of meaning that points beyond immediate circumstances. The Rig Veda emphasizes, "Those who uphold truth are led to wisdom and find stability in the eternal order" (Rig Veda 1.103.1).

In this way, satya acts as a moral compass, a guiding light that draws attention toward the ultimate source of goodness and order. It is not simply a principle to be practiced but a living presence that interacts with the human conscience, encouraging reflection, choice, and ethical engagement. Every encounter with truth, whether in thought, speech, or action, awakens an awareness that the heart longs to recognize—a reflection of the Eternal calling the human soul to participate in a life shaped by integrity, justice, and divine order.

4.3 Ahimsa – Reverence for Life

In many traditions of India the idea of *āhimsā* (अहिंसा) emerges as a profound expression of respect for life. Literally "non-injury," it grows into an ethical principle that guides thought, word, and deed. The ancient hymns of the Rig Veda speak of peace in all things: "The peace in the sky, the peace in the mid-air, the peace on earth, the peace in waters, the peace in plants, the peace in forest trees, the peace in all Gods, the peace in Brahman, the peace in peace, may that peace come to me" (Rig Veda 10.191). Such verses invite the listener to regard life itself as sacred, to act with gentleness and mindfulness rather than harm.

Ahimsa is not simply the absence of violence; it is a way of life rooted in empathy, humility, and inner transformation. In the context of the Vedic and Upanishadic vision the recognition that all beings participate in existence awakens a moral sensitivity. When one speaks gently, acts kindly, or refrains from causing injury—even unconsciously—one participates in a deeper ethos. As a commentary notes, "Do not injure the beings living on earth, in the air and in the water." (Yajur Veda) This statement points toward a holistic awareness: life in every form carries value, and our actions ripple outward beyond immediate consequence.

Practically speaking, the cultivation of ahimsa touches daily life: how one treats animals, how one uses speech, how one shapes thought. To avoid harming another is not only a social rule but an interior discipline—one monitors anger, harsh words, careless acts. When the heart becomes attentive, one begins to notice that even unkind thoughts produce disturbance. The yogic traditions list ahimsa as one of the first moral restraints, emphasizing that non-injury applies to body, speech, and mind. Through this lens, respect for life becomes a spiritual posture: the human being orients toward kindness, patience, and reverence.

Because the human heart often senses incompleteness, ahimsa functions as a mirror of something greater. When one instinctively avoids causing harm and instead acts with compassion, there is a silent acknowledgement that life is held by a power beyond human control. Ethical practices of non-injury open the way to deeper awareness—that the source of life is generous, relational, and just. The principle of ahimsa thus offers a shadow of the Eternal: life is not arbitrary, moral order is meaningful, and every creature matters.

As one practices reverence for life, sensitivity to God's presence grows. Small acts of care—listening rather than interrupting, walking rather than trampling, choosing words that heal rather than wound—become venues for spiritual formation. The heart begins to see that the same presence which sustains sun and rain also whispers in acts of kindness and silence. In this way, ahimsa is not passive withdrawal but active involvement in the flourishing of life, aligning human will with the moral rhythm of the Eternal.

Ahimsa invites the human heart to live in reverence for life—recognizing that every being reflects, in some measure, the living presence of the Creator. By practicing non-injury, empathy, and kindness, one participates in the moral and spiritual order that underlies all existence. This reverence for life prepares the soul not only for ethical living but for deeper relational encounter with God, who is the source and sustainer of every life.

4.4 The Role of Virtues in Human Formation

The cultivation of virtues is central to the spiritual and moral development emphasized in Hindu teachings. Beyond the principles of dharma, satya, and ahimsa, texts such as the Bhagavad Gita, the Upanishads, and the Dharmashastras highlight qualities like compassion, patience, forgiveness, and self-control as essential markers of a refined human heart. These virtues are not abstract ideals but practical instruments for aligning life with truth and moral order.

Compassion, or *daya* (दया), is repeatedly presented as a fundamental response to the suffering of others. The Mahabharata emphasizes that one who treats all beings with kindness and empathy experiences harmony within and contributes to the harmony of the world. The Shanti Parva of the Mahabharata states, "He who does not cause pain to any living being, whose heart is filled with compassion, is dear to all the worlds." Compassion reflects the underlying moral order and serves as a shadow of the divine care that sustains creation.

Patience, or *ksanti* (क्षान्ति), is celebrated as a virtue that stabilizes the mind and fosters discernment. The Bhagavad Gita (16:3) identifies ksanti as one of the divine qualities that elevate human conduct. Patience allows one to endure difficulty without resorting to violence, anger, or despair. By practicing patience, the human heart comes to reflect the constancy and enduring wisdom of the Eternal. The discipline of waiting and understanding shapes moral perception and prepares one to respond thoughtfully rather than impulsively.

Forgiveness, or *kshama* (क्षमा), is another virtue deeply rooted in Hindu texts. The Manusmriti (11.92) states, "The highest virtue is forgiveness, for it is the mark of the wise." Forgiveness does not merely erase wrongdoing but restores relational harmony and nurtures inner freedom. By forgiving, individuals acknowledge the limitations of human understanding while participating in a moral reality that transcends personal grievances. In practicing forgiveness, the human spirit resonates with the graciousness and patience that characterize the divine.

Self-control, or *dama* (दाम), is essential for mastery over desire and the impulses of the mind and body. The Chandogya Upanishad (7.26.2) describes the disciplined individual as one who restrains sensory indulgence and directs the mind toward higher truths. Self-control enables the cultivation of other virtues because an undisciplined mind cannot consistently act in accordance with dharma, compassion, or truth. By regulating appetite, speech, and thought, the human being gradually mirrors the deliberate, ordered, and purposeful nature of the Eternal.

Collectively, these virtues form a pattern of moral and spiritual formation. They shape the heart to perceive the world in a manner aligned with ethical and transcendent principles. Each virtue acts as a reflection or shadow of divine perfection, providing glimpses of the moral beauty inherent in the Eternal. Observing and practicing these qualities allows the human being to participate consciously in the cosmic order. They prepare the mind to recognize the fullness of divine reality while living ethically and relationally in the temporal world.

In human experience, the consistent practice of virtues brings about transformation of character and insight. One begins to perceive not only actions but intentions and underlying motivations. The cultivation of compassion, patience, forgiveness, and self-control nurtures moral discernment, allowing one to navigate the complexities of human life with wisdom and care. These virtues orient the heart toward truth and goodness, fostering an ethical vision that naturally points to a higher, personal source. In this way, virtues function as preparatory echoes of the Eternal, guiding the human soul toward fuller awareness and relational attunement with the divine.

4.5 Festivals, Rituals, and Ethical Reminder

In Hindu life, festivals and rituals are more than social or cultural celebrations. They serve as living expressions of moral and spiritual principles, guiding the individual toward dharma, satya, and ahimsa. These observances provide structured opportunities to reflect on ethical duties, spiritual truths, and relational harmony, allowing the human heart to connect with the higher reality behind ordinary life.

Festivals such as Diwali, Holi, and Navaratri are rich with moral symbolism. Diwali, the festival of lights, celebrates the victory of knowledge over ignorance and good over evil. Lighting lamps during Diwali symbolizes the illumination of conscience and ethical awareness, inviting participants to reflect on their own actions and cultivate virtue. Holi, with its vibrant colors, signifies unity, forgiveness, and renewal of relationships. Participants are encouraged to release grudges and embrace harmony, embodying the principle of ahimsa in interpersonal life. Navaratri, a festival honoring the divine feminine, emphasizes devotion, discipline, and moral reflection, encouraging practices such as fasting, prayer, and meditation to strengthen the alignment of personal life with dharma.

Rituals within daily and seasonal observances also cultivate ethical consciousness. The Sandhyavandanam, a ritual performed at dawn and dusk, combines recitation, meditation, and offerings, creating a rhythm of self-reflection and awareness of one's moral duties. The Agnihotra, the Vedic fire ritual, is not only an act of offering but also a reminder of interconnection, responsibility, and reverence for all life. The Yajurveda and Rigveda contain detailed prescriptions for these rituals, illustrating how disciplined practice fosters mindfulness and ethical sensitivity.

Through these practices, individuals are invited to participate consciously in the moral and spiritual order. Rituals encode abstract principles into lived experience, making dharma tangible in daily life. By offering attention, intention, and devotion, practitioners internalize the lessons of truth and non-violence. The Upanishads also reflect on the importance of ritual as a preparatory form, emphasizing that external observances can guide the mind toward ethical reflection and higher knowledge when performed with sincerity and understanding.

Festivals and rituals cultivate a sense of awe and gratitude, reminding participants that human life is part of a larger moral and cosmic order. They awaken the heart to the presence of the Eternal, not as an abstract idea but as a guiding reality that informs choices, relationships, and conduct. Observing the cycle of celebrations, one sees the recurring patterns of justice, compassion, and relational care, reinforcing the connection between human actions and higher ethical ideals.

In daily life, these practices encourage introspection and moral attentiveness. By observing the rhythm of festivals, participating in rites, and meditating on the symbolic meaning of rituals, the heart gradually attunes to the underlying ethical principles. Rituals become a mirror of dharma, a reflection of satya, and an embodiment of ahimsa. They offer gentle guidance, reminding humanity that ethical and spiritual formation is ongoing and relational. Festivals and rituals, therefore, act as moral teachers, showing that glimpses of the Eternal can be found not only in abstract reasoning but in lived, attentive, and celebratory life.

4.6 Shadows in Nature and Daily Life

Human life and the natural world provide continual hints of moral and spiritual order. In observing the behavior of people and the patterns of nature, one can discern principles that reflect the presence of the Eternal. Acts of kindness, fairness, and generosity in everyday interactions reveal an underlying sense of justice and ethical harmony. When a community cooperates to maintain peace, support the vulnerable, or honor truth, these actions mirror the moral patterns glimpsed in the Vedic teachings.

In the Rigveda, verses such as 10.191.2 celebrate mutual respect and righteousness, emphasizing that ethical behavior fosters harmony not only within human society but also within the cosmos. The Vedas frequently connect moral order with the order of the universe, suggesting that adherence to dharma in social life reflects the cosmic law, Ṛta. People who act with integrity and reverence for others are participating in this divine rhythm, aligning human behavior with universal principles.

Nature itself communicates these ethical echoes. Rivers follow their courses without fail, nourishing all life along their banks, illustrating generosity and sustenance. Trees provide shelter and fruit without demanding recognition, demonstrating quiet benevolence. Birds and animals care for their young, hunt without excess, and live within natural limits. Observing these patterns encourages humans to cultivate respect for life, patience, and cooperation. The natural world becomes a teacher of ethical attentiveness and moral reflection.

Daily life offers smaller, yet profound, reminders of the Eternal. Sharing meals, offering help to a neighbor, honoring truth in speech, and exercising restraint in desires all manifest glimpses of higher moral order. The Mahabharata frequently highlights the significance of such actions. In the Shanti Parva, it is stated that even modest acts of justice and compassion contribute to the preservation of dharma and the well-being of society. These moments of ethical attention remind the heart that moral responsibility is not abstract but woven into ordinary living.

When humans observe both nature and social life attentively, they become aware of patterns that point beyond the immediate. Reciprocity, fairness, and care for others echo the order and goodness inherent in the universe. The small acts of human conscience and the rhythms of creation together create a moral landscape, preparing the mind and heart to recognize a higher, personal source of justice, love, and truth. Through this lens, daily life becomes a canvas for seeing shadows of the Eternal, inviting reflection, gratitude, and intentional ethical living.

4.7 Yearning for the Personal and Relational God

Human experience reveals that moral and ethical ideals, while noble and illuminating, are never complete in themselves. Dharma, satya, and ahimsa guide conduct and cultivate inner harmony, yet the human heart senses a deeper longing for connection beyond the observable order. In the Vedic and Upanishadic traditions, this yearning is acknowledged as an intuitive awareness of a higher reality. The Upanishads describe this reality as both ultimate and personal, approachable through contemplation and inner listening.

The Brihadaranyaka Upanishad emphasizes the intimate aspect of the eternal, stating in 1.4.14 that the self that dwells in the heart of every being is one with the supreme. While ethical living nurtures alignment with cosmic law, it is this inner awareness of the divine self that opens the heart to relational experience. The human mind naturally seeks more than rules and principles; it desires engagement with a presence that can be known, trusted, and loved.

In daily life, this longing manifests in subtle ways. Individuals yearn for guidance when facing moral uncertainty, seek consolation in moments of sorrow, and experience joy in shared love and service. The Mahabharata illustrates this desire for divine companionship in numerous passages. In the Bhishma Parva, warriors and sages alike turn inward for counsel and reassurance, indicating that ethical living alone is insufficient without recognition of a guiding, personal presence.

The Upanishads often contrast shadows of wisdom and the fullness of the eternal reality. Living according to dharma, observing truth, and practicing non-violence provide glimpses of moral perfection, but they remain incomplete without the relational and personal engagement of the divine. The Svetasvatara Upanishad 6.9 describes meditation upon the supreme being as a means to realize the ultimate, who not only upholds creation but also engages personally with the devotee. Ethical ideals orient the heart, but the fullness of love, guidance, and relational intimacy comes from recognizing a personal God.

This awareness shapes human longing. The heart naturally seeks communion, not mere adherence to law. Love, trust, and attentive listening arise from this relational yearning. Every act of moral awareness or ethical choice awakens the sense that life is incomplete without the personal presence of the Eternal, whose care and guidance surpass the shadows of virtue alone. The ethical and moral framework of Hindu thought, while illuminating, points forward to the fullness of relational encounter that can satisfy the deepest human need for connection, guidance, and love.

4.8 Moral Intuition as a Guide

The human conscience functions as a subtle compass, guiding decisions and revealing the contours of right and wrong even when formal instruction is absent. In Hindu thought, this intuitive awareness is closely linked to the notion of dharma, not merely as external duty but as an inner recognition of what is proper and just. The Manusmriti, for example, speaks of an inner understanding of righteousness, indicating that ethical discernment is not solely dependent on law but is accessible through attentive reflection and moral sensitivity.

Vedic literature also acknowledges this inner moral sense. The Brihadaranyaka Upanishad emphasizes that self-awareness and introspection cultivate the discernment to perceive truth and act rightly. By attending to the voice within, one perceives the deeper order of life. This moral intuition mirrors the Eternal's guiding presence and allows individuals to navigate ethical dilemmas with wisdom and integrity.

Human experience confirms this guidance. Even in cultures without systematic theology, people recognize that certain acts resonate with conscience, producing a sense of peace, while other actions disturb the mind and heart. This natural alignment suggests that the Eternal has implanted a recognition of truth and goodness within the human soul. In the Bhagavad Gita 3.35, Krishna instructs Arjuna to perform duty in accordance with his nature and conscience, emphasizing that following this inner guidance aligns the individual with the divine order.

Moral intuition is not static; it is cultivated through reflection, observation, and disciplined practice. By listening attentively, humans learn to distinguish between fleeting desires and enduring principles. Acts of honesty, kindness, and compassion reinforce the capacity to hear the subtle promptings of conscience. Each moment of moral choice is an encounter with the shadows of the Eternal, suggesting the fuller reality that awaits relational engagement with God.

Ethical insight is also relational. Observing the consequences of actions on others sharpens moral perception, revealing patterns of justice, mercy, and care that are consistent across cultures. The Mahabharata, in multiple passages, illustrates how warriors and sages follow inner guidance to act rightly, showing that conscience is a shared human faculty pointing beyond immediate circumstances toward a universal moral order.

Listening to conscience aligns the heart with truth and goodness that transcends personal preference. This moral awareness forms a bridge between human ethical practice and the relational presence of the Eternal. It prepares the soul to recognize the fullness of divine guidance, which is not merely prescriptive but inviting, intimate, and transformative. Moral intuition offers a steady whisper of the Eternal, shaping thought, guiding action, and nurturing the longing for complete communion with the divine.

4.9 Shadows as Preparation for Revelation

The ethical and spiritual ideals found in Hindu scriptures offer more than moral guidance; they serve as early preparations for encountering the fullness of divine revelation. Practices such as living according to dharma, speaking truth in alignment with satya, and honoring life through ahimsa cultivate sensitivity in the heart and mind. This cultivation allows the human spirit to recognize when the Eternal reveals Himself more personally and directly. In the Brihadaranyaka Upanishad, the pursuit of knowledge and virtue is portrayed as a way of purifying the mind and attuning oneself to a reality that transcends ordinary perception. The seeker learns to perceive patterns of harmony, justice, and care as signs that point beyond immediate appearances toward a deeper source.

The glimpses of the Eternal found in moral and ethical practice act as guiding lights. The human heart, when attentive to conscience and relational virtues, begins to anticipate the living presence that these shadows foreshadow. In the Bhagavad Gita 13.7, Krishna describes knowledge, discernment, and humility as pathways that elevate the soul toward understanding the ultimate. The cultivation of these virtues trains the heart to discern the voice of the Word and to recognize the light of truth when it appears more fully. Shadows in moral and spiritual practice awaken expectation, forming a context in which revelation can be received with openness and clarity.

Observing ethical patterns in daily life also prepares the seeker for the relational aspect of God. Acts of justice, kindness, and integrity are not only expressions of human virtue but also signs that the world itself carries an orientation toward the Eternal. The human capacity to sense incompleteness, to long for what is just, true, and good, mirrors the soul's readiness to encounter the Word made flesh. This anticipation is reflected in the Upanishads, where the seeker's devotion, reflection, and ethical striving are described as leading toward a personal realization of Brahman, the ultimate reality.

The principle of preparation through shadows extends to human awareness of the relational nature of God. When one recognizes the limits of ethical and spiritual ideals, it generates a natural desire for a presence that fulfills them completely. The moral and spiritual shadows experienced in life awaken receptivity, guiding the seeker to the fullness of divine truth. Human conscience, disciplined by virtue and reflection, becomes a lens through which the clarity and relational presence of God can be discerned when it is revealed.

The shadows of ethical, moral, and spiritual practice therefore act as a preparatory path. They do not offer completion but invite the heart toward fulfillment. The glimpses of the Eternal in duty, truth, and compassion encourage the human spirit to recognize that these virtues are reflections of something greater. As the seeker progresses in attentiveness, the shadows of moral insight gradually illuminate the path, fostering the inner readiness to encounter the Word who embodies ultimate truth, goodness, and relational love.

Conclusion: Living in the Light of What is Coming

The ethical and spiritual ideals found within Hindu teachings serve as profound indicators of the Eternal, offering the human heart early glimpses of what is ultimate. Dharma, as the path of righteous living, provides structure and guidance for daily conduct. It fosters harmony within the self and in society, reflecting an underlying moral order that hints at a higher reality. Satya, the commitment to truth, aligns human speech and thought with a reality that surpasses immediate perception. By honoring truth in daily life, the seeker participates in a larger, universal order that reflects the character of the Eternal. Ahimsa nurtures respect and reverence for life, cultivating empathy and relational sensitivity. Practices such as forgiveness, patience, and self-restraint develop moral discernment and shape the heart toward goodness and relational integrity. The Upanishads, including the Brihadaranyaka and Chandogya, describe these virtues as preparatory steps toward understanding Brahman, the ultimate reality that unites moral insight with relational presence.

The human heart, when attentive to these ideals, naturally senses incompleteness without the fullness of God. Every act of ethical awareness, every decision to align with truth and compassion, awakens a longing for the One who is the source and fulfillment of all goodness. Observing the shadows of the Eternal in daily life—through acts of kindness, honesty, justice, and care—prepares the spirit to receive the ultimate revelation of God in history. The moral and spiritual patterns embedded in culture, scripture, and human interaction function as signposts, pointing beyond the finite toward the infinite. The Bhagavad Gita emphasizes that knowledge, discernment, and devotion elevate the soul, cultivating readiness to recognize the ultimate reality when it appears in fullness.

Living in anticipation shapes human experience in profound ways. Awareness of these glimpses encourages humility, attentiveness, and gratitude, forming the heart to respond with openness to God's presence. Each moral and spiritual effort becomes a form of preparation, training the conscience and imagination to recognize the divine when it is made manifest. Ethical reflection and spiritual cultivation are not ends in themselves but invitations to participate in a relationship with the Eternal who fulfills every longing of the human spirit. The shadows of dharma, satya, ahimsa, and other virtues awaken expectation, drawing the heart toward the Word who is the source of life, light, and truth.

Readers are invited to reflect on these questions: Where do you sense the shadow of the Eternal in your life? Which virtues, practices, or moral ideals draw your heart toward God? Observing these indications of the Eternal encourages attentiveness and shapes the inner disposition for the coming revelation. Living in the light of what is coming is a journey of expectation, ethical engagement, and spiritual sensitivity, where the human heart learns to recognize the preparation already present within daily life as a foretaste of the fullness of God.

Part III — The Fullness Revealed in Christ

The search of humanity reaches its completion in the revelation of Jesus Christ. The long journey of the human heart, which began with wonder and continued through moral discovery, finds its destination in the Eternal Word made flesh. In Christ, the mystery of truth, goodness, and divine presence is revealed not as an abstract idea but as a living relationship. The unseen becomes visible, the infinite becomes personal, and the longing of the soul finds rest in the grace of God who enters human history.

Part III of this work unfolds the great theme of fulfillment. The earlier chapters traced humanity's intuition of the Eternal through creation, conscience, and moral reflection. Now the focus turns to the revelation of God in Christ, where divine truth assumes human form. The Son of God becomes the bridge between heaven and earth, revealing the heart of the Father through His life, teaching, death, and resurrection. Every symbol, every virtue, and every shadow of truth throughout history finds meaning in Him.

The chapters of this section guide the reader through this sacred realization. The first examines the deep longing for a Savior that has existed in every culture, showing how humanity's cry for redemption meets its answer in divine compassion. The following chapter presents Christ as the eternal Word through whom all things were made, the light that illumines both reason and spirit. The next reflections explore the life that flows from this revelation, where divine love transforms the believer's inner being and renews every relationship. The final chapter in this part portrays the response of faith, as the heart that encounters Christ moves from seeking to surrender, from curiosity to communion.

This section affirms that Jesus Christ embodies the fullness of all that humanity has sought through ages. The divine that the sages glimpsed and the prophets foretold is revealed completely in Him. Through His incarnation, the Eternal enters time; through His cross, grace triumphs over guilt; through His resurrection, life conquers death. The revelation of Christ is therefore the center of all truth and the completion of every genuine spiritual quest.

Part III invites the reader to contemplate this mystery with both awe and gratitude. It presents faith not as the abandonment of human inquiry but as its fulfillment.

Chapter 5: The Longing for the One Who Saves

From the very beginning, human beings have felt a profound sense of incompleteness. Life offers many forms of satisfaction, yet the heart often senses a need that cannot be met by wealth, power, or worldly achievements. This deep yearning extends beyond mere survival or comfort; it touches the moral, emotional, and spiritual dimensions of existence. Across cultures and ages, people have recognized a longing for protection, guidance, forgiveness, and enduring love that transcends what the material world can provide.

In the Bhagavad Gita, Krishna speaks to Arjuna about the necessity of divine intervention for the preservation of righteousness and the restoration of balance. In chapter 4, verses 7 and 8, Krishna declares that whenever dharma wanes and adharma rises, the Divine incarnates to protect the good, destroy the wicked, and reestablish cosmic order. This illustrates that the human heart, aware of its own limitations and the imperfections of the world, naturally looks beyond itself toward a source of ultimate justice and care. It is not merely an intellectual curiosity or abstract desire; it is a relational call for one who actively engages with the human condition.

Human experience provides countless examples of this longing. A child seeking reassurance in the night, a person asking for guidance in a moment of moral uncertainty, or an individual yearning for forgiveness after failing to live up to ethical ideals—all reveal the innate orientation of the human heart toward a personal source of help and love. The desire for protection is not selfishness but reflects the understanding that life is fragile, moral choice is challenging, and human imperfection is universal.

Forgiveness is another dimension of this longing. People recognize that they cannot perfect themselves through effort alone. Remorse and repentance arise naturally when one reflects on actions that harm others or compromise moral ideals. The human conscience is like a compass, sensing what is right yet incapable of delivering absolute reconciliation. The Gita's depiction of Krishna acting for the preservation of dharma shows that the Eternal responds to human longing, restoring harmony when individuals or society fail to uphold justice.

Love, as a final dimension, represents the deepest yearning. Material provisions can meet immediate needs, but enduring love requires recognition, care, and relational commitment. The human heart seeks a love that is unwavering, responsive, and intimately connected with moral and spiritual well-being. This yearning points to a relational God whose concern is personal rather than abstract, and whose engagement with humanity is active rather than distant.

Reflective questions arise naturally from this understanding. When do you feel the deepest longing for guidance or protection? Where do you notice the limitations of human solutions and the need for something beyond yourself? How does your conscience and emotional awareness hint at a source of ultimate goodness and care? These questions prepare the heart for considering not only divine action in texts like the Gita but also the fuller revelation of God entering human history in the person of Christ.

Human longing, therefore, is more than desire; it is an orientation of the soul toward a source capable of addressing moral imperfection, relational needs, and the spiritual hunger that no worldly solution can satisfy. It is an invitation to recognize that ethical ideals and glimpses of righteousness, while significant, point to one who fully embodies and fulfills them. In every longing for protection, guidance, forgiveness, or love, the human heart carries the memory of the Eternal and the anticipation of the One who saves.

5.1 Human Longing as a Reflection of the Eternal

Human longing is an intrinsic part of our existence. From early childhood, people sense desires that go beyond immediate gratification, reaching toward something enduring and meaningful. These desires are not only emotional but also ethical and relational. When a person experiences conscience stirring in response to a moral choice, when empathy moves the heart to care for another, or when love seeks connection, there emerges a reflection of a reality that surpasses the self. This innate longing indicates that the human heart is attuned to the eternal and relational dimensions of life.

The ethical ideals explored in the previous chapter, such as dharma, satya, and ahimsa, reveal the same pattern. Dharma, understood as the path of righteous living, aligns the individual with a moral order that seems to originate from a source beyond human construction. Satya, the pursuit of truth, awakens an awareness that honesty and alignment with reality carry spiritual weight. Ahimsa, or reverence for life, points to a relational ethic that values care and respect across creation. While these ideals illuminate the path toward virtue, they remain shadows, incomplete without the presence of the one who can fulfill them. They prepare the heart to recognize that the fulfillment of these longings exists in a personal, relational God rather than in abstract principles alone.

Throughout human history, stories reveal how longing manifests in everyday experience. Consider the hope of a parent for the well-being of a child, or the aspiration of a student striving for moral integrity amid social pressures. The grief and regret that follow ethical failures underscore the heart's awareness of imperfection and the need for restoration. In literature, poetry, and oral traditions across cultures, themes of yearning, unfulfilled desire, and pursuit of justice echo the recognition that humans are oriented toward an ideal they cannot fully attain on their own.

The Bhagavad Gita offers a clear example of this interplay between human longing and divine action. In chapter 4, verses 7 and 8, Krishna describes the divine response to the decline of dharma: whenever ethical and moral decay appears, the Divine intervenes to restore balance and protect the righteous. This action reflects an intimate engagement with human longing, demonstrating that the Eternal responds to the imperfection and desire for justice within human hearts. People are called to recognize not only the limitations of their own efforts but also the loving provision of the one who actively engages in history to fulfill what they cannot accomplish alone.

Human longing, therefore, is simultaneously personal and universal. It is personal in its expression through conscience, desire, and relational awareness. It is universal because all human beings, regardless of culture or time, sense incompleteness and seek fulfillment in truth, love, and moral goodness. These longings act as indicators pointing toward the Eternal, revealing a heart naturally oriented to receive divine guidance, restoration, and relational intimacy.

The reflection of the Eternal in human longing provides both hope and humility. Hope arises because the heart's desires are not accidental; they are invitations to encounter a reality beyond the visible and temporal. Humility arises because human effort alone cannot satisfy the depth of these yearnings. Recognizing this creates an openness to a savior, one who fulfills not only ethical and moral ideals but also the personal and relational needs that define the human experience.

Stories from daily life provide constant reminders of this dynamic. When someone forgives an enemy, comforts a grieving friend, or acts courageously in the face of injustice, the heart experiences a resonance with the Eternal's love and justice. In every act that reflects the ethical shadows from Chapter 4, the longing for a deeper fulfillment becomes apparent. These longing invites individuals to look beyond themselves, to sense the presence of one who can meet the heart fully, and to anticipate the arrival of the one who saves.

5.2 Divine Intervention in Krishna's Teaching

The Bhagavad Gita provides a profound insight into the nature of divine action within the human story. In chapter 4, verses 7 and 8, Krishna speaks of the recurring need for the Divine to enter the world whenever unrighteousness increases and the moral order declines. He assures that the Eternal manifests personally to protect the virtuous, restore dharma, and guide humanity back toward justice and spiritual harmony. This teaching emphasizes that divine intervention is rooted in care and relational engagement, not merely abstract judgment.

Krishna's words highlight an aspect of God that resonates deeply with the human heart: the Divine does not leave creation to drift amid moral chaos. The intervention is purposeful and compassionate. Human beings, in the midst of struggle, despair, or confusion, encounter assurance that they are not alone. Ethical ideals such as dharma, satya, and ahimsa, while vital, can be challenging to maintain in a world fraught with complexity and moral ambiguity. Krishna's teaching reflects a reality where the Eternal steps into human history, offering guidance, protection, and restoration when human effort alone falls short.

The Gita frames divine action not as mere reaction to wrongdoing, but as a restorative presence that nurtures life and moral order. When Krishna acts, the focus is on preserving the framework that allows ethical living to flourish. The goal is not to punish indiscriminately, but to uphold righteousness, safeguard the virtuous, and provide the means for ethical and spiritual growth. Human beings, encountering this truth, can perceive that divine action is relational and concerned with human well-being. It models a God who engages with the human condition in a personal and empathetic manner, attuned to both moral realities and human fragility.

This perspective on divine intervention also carries spiritual implications for personal life. It demonstrates that ethical and moral struggle does not occur in isolation from divine attention. The guidance offered by Krishna encourages reflection on the human need for support, correction, and alignment with eternal truth. One is reminded that spiritual formation is a cooperative journey: human responsibility is met with divine accompaniment. Moral perseverance is strengthened by the knowledge that the Eternal seeks to restore, protect, and uplift rather than condemn for its own sake.

Stories of human experience mirror this dynamic. People facing crises—whether ethical dilemmas, relational conflicts, or moments of personal failure—often sense an unseen presence guiding them toward restoration. The human conscience, when it perceives a higher call to truth and justice, resonates with the principle Krishna articulates. Ethical lapses are met with opportunity for redemption, and moral courage is reinforced by an understanding that the Divine supports those striving to live rightly.

Krishna's teaching thus reveals a model of God as active, relational, and redemptive. It portrays divine intervention as deeply personal, responding to the real needs of the human heart and moral life. In doing so, it prepares individuals to receive the greater fulfillment of these longings in the one who saves, the incarnation who embodies the Eternal Word. Through this lens, human experience of struggle, hope, and ethical striving is never wasted, for it points toward a God who acts decisively to restore righteousness and cultivate life that aligns with the eternal order.

5.3 Longing for Forgiveness and Transformation

The human heart carries an innate awareness of imperfection. Even those who strive to live ethically experience moments of failure, regret, and guilt. This awareness generates a profound longing for forgiveness, a desire to reconcile with what has been broken in life and relationships. Across cultures and religious traditions, this inner ache is recognized as a signal of the soul's need for restoration. In Hindu thought, the practice of self-reflection and confession, seen in rituals of repentance and penance, acknowledges the gap between human imperfection and the moral order. Scriptures such as the Manusmriti and the Upanishads describe processes of ethical and spiritual correction, emphasizing that sincere recognition of wrongdoing opens the path to inner renewal.

Forgiveness is not only an ethical act but also a transformative one. When individuals experience forgiveness, they are invited into moral and spiritual healing that restores integrity and aligns the heart with truth. This longing for reconciliation reflects a deeper anticipation: the desire for an agent who can mediate between human imperfection and divine order. The conscience, aware of its own limitations, seeks relief from the burden of guilt while yearning to live in harmony with eternal principles. Repentance and remorse, therefore, become more than private acts; they are signs of a soul reaching for restoration and relational fullness.

In lived human experience, these moments of longing are deeply personal. A person who has wronged another may seek reconciliation, understanding that moral and relational wholeness cannot be achieved alone. Similarly, one who has failed to live according to conscience senses a need for restoration that transcends mere self-effort. Historical accounts and scriptural narratives repeatedly illustrate that humans seek a savior who addresses both ethical failure and relational disruption. The Psalms, for instance, express heartfelt pleas for forgiveness and renewal, highlighting a pattern of human longing that transcends time and culture.

Anticipation of a savior is thus rooted in both conscience and relationship. Ethical ideals and moral striving create awareness of human limitations, while relational desires highlight the need for a personal, responsive presence. The human heart does not merely seek correction or moral instruction but desires engagement with a being who offers true reconciliation. Forgiveness, in this sense, is inseparable from transformation: it restores the moral self and invites participation in a fuller life aligned with the Eternal.

Experiences of remorse, repentance, and seeking moral wholeness reveal the soul's readiness to receive divine intervention. The longing for forgiveness is an opening of the heart, an invitation for restoration that anticipates the one who saves. This yearning, cultivated through reflection, ethical striving, and relational awareness, forms the foundation for encountering the fulfillment of human expectation in the Word made flesh, who alone reconciles conscience, restores relationships, and transforms hearts toward enduring life and love.

5.4 Divine Love as Invitation, Not Coercion

Human experience shows that true guidance flourishes only when it is freely received. The heart resists force, but it responds to genuine care, wisdom, and relational engagement. This principle is evident in the divine action portrayed in the Bhagavad Gita. In chapter 4, verses 7 and 8, Krishna steps into the human situation not as a tyrant but as one who restores righteousness with discernment and mercy. He does not compel Arjuna to act mechanically; rather, he illuminates the path, explains duty, and invites understanding.

The divine presence respects human freedom while offering the clarity and support needed to choose rightly.

Krishna's engagement demonstrates that divine love operates through invitation. The emphasis is on relational connection rather than imposition. Guidance is offered in a way that nurtures insight, encourages reflection, and inspires ethical action. In human terms, it resembles a teacher who does not merely dictate rules but inspires learning through patient explanation and exemplification. By observing moral order and participating in virtuous action, the individual is drawn into alignment with the Eternal, yet the choice remains personal.

This approach has spiritual and psychological implications. When God invites rather than coerces, the human heart experiences both security and freedom. Trust is cultivated through relational interaction, and moral growth occurs through conscious assent rather than fear. By inviting the soul to respond, divine love fosters internal transformation, shaping conscience, character, and relational sensitivity.

Reflective openness becomes a key posture for encountering the divine. The heart, aware of its own longing for restoration and guidance, can respond to God's invitation with trust, attentiveness, and moral engagement. In this relational dynamic, divine action and human response are intertwined. Krishna's example illustrates that God's presence in history is not a distant imposition but an accessible, relational reality. Through wisdom, mercy, and careful guidance, God calls the heart to participate in moral order, ethical living, and ultimately, communion with the Eternal.

5.5 Preparing the Heart for Christ

The human heart, having glimpsed moral and spiritual ideals and experienced the invitation of divine love, naturally moves toward a deeper fulfillment. Krishna's action in the Gita illustrates that God enters human history to restore righteousness and provide guidance. This prepares the mind and heart to recognize a greater revelation, the one who fulfills the longings that moral ideals and ethical shadows can only hint at. Christ, as the Word made flesh, embodies the perfect alignment of love, truth, and relational guidance, meeting the heart where its yearning is most profound.

Ethical and spiritual readiness plays a crucial role in this encounter. The seeker's attention must be cultivated, learning to perceive the subtle promptings of conscience and the moral order evident in daily life. Humility opens the heart to receive instruction, acknowledging that human effort alone cannot achieve fullness. Desire for truth and beauty, which appears in the pursuit of dharma, satya, and ahimsa, attunes the soul to the voice of God calling in history. Openness to love allows one to recognize not only ethical correctness but the relational presence of God active in the world.

In the Gospel of John, the coming of Christ is portrayed as the arrival of the eternal Word into human experience. Those whose hearts have been prepared by moral insight, ethical longing, and relational awareness are positioned to recognize the significance of this arrival. Christ does not force recognition, but the attentive and responsive heart discerns the fullness of God's saving work. Through reflection, prayer, and a conscious orientation toward truth and love, the human heart becomes a receptive space for divine encounter.

Engagement with spiritual and ethical life, inspired by glimpses of God in creation and moral ideals, sets the stage for this relational fulfillment. By fostering attentiveness, humility, and desire, the seeker is ready to participate in the transformation Christ brings. The longings of conscience and heart, shaped by shadows and invitations, find their true object in the Word who speaks, guides, and restores life in a personal and relational way.

5.6 Human Longing and the Promise of Salvation

The human heart carries a persistent desire for life that is secure, for guidance that is trustworthy, and for reconciliation that heals brokenness. Across cultures and eras, people experience an awareness of their own limitations and a sense that worldly means cannot fully satisfy the deep yearnings of the soul. This longing is neither accidental nor trivial; it reveals an innate orientation toward something greater than ourselves. Ethical instincts, moral awareness, and relational desires all point beyond human effort to the One who can truly restore and fulfill.

The promise of salvation finds resonance in this universal yearning. In the teachings of the Bhagavad Gita, Krishna assures the seeker that divine intervention occurs to restore dharma and guide humanity toward righteousness. The moral and spiritual call that humans sense naturally anticipates a response from the Eternal, one who acts not coercively, but out of love and relational care. This yearning becomes a guide, directing attention and aspiration toward the fullness of life promised in the Word made flesh.

Every individual experiences longing uniquely. For some it arises in the quiet of reflection, in the search for ethical clarity or in the desire for reconciliation with others. For others it appears in moments of awe before nature, the recognition of beauty, or the experience of mercy received. Across these experiences, human hearts reveal a pattern: longing is not merely personal; it is also universal, reflecting a shared orientation toward God. Attentive awareness of this inner movement prepares the soul to recognize salvation when it enters history, offering hope, restoration, and intimate relational encounter with the Eternal.

Reflection and Invitation

Take a moment to notice the stirrings of your own heart. Where do you feel a deep need for protection, guidance, or unconditional love? Consider the ways in which experiences of mercy, forgiveness, or ethical clarity have touched your conscience and awakened a sense of the divine. These moments, whether subtle or profound, are signposts pointing toward the one who fulfills what the heart has long sought.

Observe the ways moral intuition moves you to act rightly even when external authority is absent. Reflect on the relational desires that drive your decisions, the longing to reconcile with others, or to live with integrity and compassion. These instincts reveal a sensitivity to something greater than mere human effort. They prepare the heart to recognize the Savior when the Word enters human history, inviting participation in a relationship that satisfies the deepest longings.

Notice how your spiritual yearning emerges in everyday life, in quiet reflection, in prayer, or in the pursuit of justice and care for others. These glimpses of righteousness, mercy, and love shape awareness and open the soul to receive what has been promised. Attentive observation of these inner movements transforms ordinary experiences into preparation, inviting the heart to meet the Eternal, who offers salvation, guidance, and enduring relational presence.

Chapter 6: The Eternal Word Becomes Flesh

Human hearts have always carried an innate sense of longing, a quiet yearning for truth, goodness, and beauty that seems larger than any one human life. In Chapter 4, we explored how moral ideals, ethical principles, and spiritual intuitions in Hindu thought—dharma, satya, ahimsa, and other virtues—act as glimpses or shadows of a higher reality. These ideals point toward something beyond themselves, suggesting that the human soul is naturally drawn to a fullness that ethical living alone cannot completely satisfy.

Throughout history, people have sensed that morality, conscience, and spiritual insight are not arbitrary. They respond to a higher law, a moral architecture, or a divine rhythm woven into the fabric of existence. The Vedas and Upanishads echo this awareness. The Mundaka Upanishad states that through knowing Brahman, one transcends ignorance and attains liberation. The Śvetāśvatara Upanishad also presents the personal aspect of the divine, hinting that there is a presence that responds to devotion and contemplation. Even when human understanding is limited to shadows, the heart perceives that these glimpses point toward something fuller.

This longing for relational encounter is universal. In all cultures, human beings have looked beyond themselves for guidance, inspiration, and meaning. The ethical ideals that guide daily life are not merely social conventions; they are responses to the whispers of the Eternal that stir the human heart. They suggest the existence of a reality that is personal, relational, and deeply involved in human affairs. People sense that goodness, truth, and compassion originate from a source that is more than the human mind can produce.

The transition from ethical shadows and intuitive insights to the full revelation of God in history raises profound questions. How does the Eternal move from symbol, shadow, and ideal into human history in a way that can be known personally? What does it mean for the Eternal Word to dwell among people, not only as a principle or ideal but as a living presence who speaks, acts, and invites relationship? The Gospel of John provides a clear answer, introducing the Word who is both eternal and personal, who enters history to fulfill the longings already present in the human heart.

The human yearning, cultivated through moral reflection, conscience, and spiritual awareness, is thus not in vain. It prepares the heart for recognition and encounter with the Word made flesh. Every moral insight, every act of compassion, every pursuit of truth in human life points forward to the One who embodies these ideals perfectly. The shadows of dharma, satya, and ahimsa anticipate a reality where goodness is fully incarnated, where truth is not only known but embodied, and where the human soul meets the Eternal in personal, relational encounter.

In this chapter, we will trace this movement from the anticipatory shadows to the full revelation of the Eternal Word in Jesus Christ. We will explore how the Logos becomes accessible to human experience, how the divine light and truth enter history, and how the relational presence of God addresses the yearnings of every heart that has ever sought the Eternal. We will reflect on how ethical ideals and moral intuitions serve as preparation, guiding the human spirit toward recognition of the living Word who walks among us.

The questions remain for each reader to consider: How do your own ethical choices, your conscience, and your desire for truth point beyond the immediate and material world? In what ways do the longings you carry echo the eternal call of the Word who comes to dwell among us? These reflections open the heart to the anticipation of fulfillment, creating a space for the mystery of the Eternal Word to be encountered personally in history.

6.1 The Logos Revealed in History

The Gospel of John opens with words that have echoed through the centuries, revealing the eternal and relational nature of the Logos. In John 1:1-3, it is written, "In the beginning was the Word, and the Word was with God, and the Word was God. He was in the beginning with God. All things were made through Him, and without Him nothing was made that has been made." These verses emphasize that the Logos is not an abstract principle but a living presence intimately involved in the very fabric of reality. The eternal Word existed before creation, yet the Word's relation to humanity is intentional and personal.

When the Logos enters history, as described in John 1:14, the eternal Word becomes flesh and dwells among us. The text states, "The Word became flesh and made his dwelling among us. We have seen his glory, the glory of the one and only Son, who came from the Father, full of grace and truth." Here, the divine is no longer only hinted at through ethical principles or moral insight but is concretely present in the person of Jesus Christ. Humanity, which has long glimpsed shadows of truth, justice, and compassion through conscience and dharmic ideals, now encounters the fullness of what those glimpses anticipated. Ethical yearnings and moral awareness find their living fulfillment in the relational presence of the Logos. This historical revelation contrasts with prior glimpses of the divine in Hindu thought. Virtues such as dharma, satya, and ahimsa provide guidance and reflection, echoing the moral order of the cosmos as described in the Upanishads and the Vedas. They awaken the heart to the possibility of harmony with the Eternal. Yet these glimpses, while profound, remain anticipatory. The Logos in history embodies what morality and conscience have always pointed toward. The human longing for ultimate justice, truth, and relational intimacy with the divine is met not as a distant ideal but as a tangible presence who walks among people, teaches, heals, and calls hearts into transformation.

History itself becomes a stage of divine communication. The actions, words, and life of Jesus reveal the character and intentions of God in ways that ethical reflection alone cannot. In His teachings, parables, and encounters, the eternal Word shows how moral and spiritual principles are lived in human experience. People witnessing these events encountered divine truth in action. Historical moments, sacred narratives, and the unfolding of human events are imbued with significance because the Logos is actively engaging with creation. The Gospel presents this interaction as relational rather than coercive. The Word invites response, guidance, and communion rather than demanding passive acknowledgment.

Human experience resonates with this revelation because the heart has always been attuned to the eternal. The moral intuitions, ethical reflections, and yearning for relational intimacy with the divine, present across cultures and highlighted in Hindu moral thought, now find a living fulfillment. Individuals encounter the Logos through teaching, action, and presence. John 1:16 explains that from Christ's fullness, we have all received grace upon grace. The relational aspect is emphasized: knowing the Word is not merely intellectual understanding but involves trust, response, and alignment with divine intention.

Through the Logos in history, the Eternal is no longer an abstract guiding principle but a personal companion. The eternal Word provides moral clarity, relational depth, and spiritual fulfillment in human experience. Where ethical and spiritual ideals prepared the heart, historical revelation actualizes what the soul has long desired. By entering history, the Word bridges the gap between shadow and reality, between ethical aspiration and divine encounter, demonstrating that the human search for truth, goodness, and relational presence finds its ultimate answer in Jesus Christ.

6.2 Christ as Word and Light

In the Gospel of John, Christ is presented as both the Word and the Light, fully embodying the eternal Logos in human form. John 1:4–5 states, "In him was life, and that life was the light of all mankind. The light shines in the darkness, and the darkness has not overcome it." This light is not merely physical illumination but a spiritual and moral clarity that guides understanding, awakens conscience, and invites human hearts into relationship with God. Christ speaks, acts, and reveals truth, offering guidance that engages both mind and heart.

The identity of Christ as Word connects directly with the Vāk discussed in Chapter 2, yet now it is fully personal and historical. Where Vāk was understood as an inner awareness guiding thought and conscience, the Logos incarnate communicates directly, teaching with authority, calling disciples, and demonstrating divine wisdom through action. In Matthew 4:19, Jesus calls Peter and Andrew to follow him, saying, "Follow me, and I will make you fishers of men." Here, the Word addresses individuals, inviting response and forming community. The abstract principle of moral truth becomes a relational call, demonstrating how divine speech transforms lives in real time.

Christ as Light also illuminates human understanding. In John 8:12, Jesus declares, "I am the light of the world. Whoever follows me will never walk in darkness, but will have the light of life." This illumination is practical and relational. It guides moral perception, reveals the nature of God's love, and provides discernment in ethical and spiritual decisions. Just as inner light awakens conscience, the incarnate Light shows the path of grace, forgiveness, and relational intimacy with God. Human experience of this light is active: it invites reflection, ethical alignment, and attentive response.

Gospel narratives further illustrate how Christ embodies both Word and Light. Through healing, parables, and personal encounters, Jesus reveals the moral and spiritual order of God's kingdom. In Luke 7:22, the works of Jesus—healing the sick and proclaiming good news—demonstrate how divine speech and presence operate in history. Each act communicates care, restores wholeness, and illuminates truth in human experience. The Word is not abstract theory; it is alive, engaging the senses, emotions, and intellect.

Relationally, the Word and Light are intertwined. Christ speaks not to dominate but to invite, not to impose but to guide. Ethical principles, moral intuition, and human longing for truth now meet the fullness of relational encounter. The personal communication of the Logos nurtures understanding, calls for response, and transforms daily life. The Light exposes what is hidden, clarifies what is uncertain, and inspires moral courage. Those who receive this Word and Light find their conscience, heart, and life aligned with God's presence in practical and relational ways.

Through the revelation of Christ as Word and Light, the human longing for clarity, guidance, and relational intimacy with the Eternal is fulfilled. Ethical shadows, moral ideals, and the intuitive sense of truth from prior human experience now converge in personal encounter with Jesus. The Word speaks, the Light illumines, and hearts are invited to respond with trust, discernment, and devotion. History itself becomes a medium for divine communication, bridging the eternal and temporal, the ideal and the realized, guiding humanity toward fullness in God's relational presence.

6.3 The Relational Presence of God

The revelation of Christ as the Eternal Word emphasizes that God's presence is fundamentally relational. God is not a distant moral ideal or an abstract principle but a personal companion who engages with the human heart. Jesus demonstrates this intimacy through speech, action, and sustained presence, showing that ethical life is inseparable from relationship with the Divine. In John 15:15, Jesus tells his disciples, "I no longer call you servants, because a servant does not know his master's business. Instead, I have called you friends, for everything that I learned from my Father I have made known to you." Here, relational knowledge becomes the key to understanding God's will and purpose.

Human response to this relational presence requires trust, love, and obedience grounded in relationship rather than mere rule-following. Ethical principles such as dharma, satya, and ahimsa, explored in earlier chapters, now find their completion in relational practice. Living according to these moral ideals becomes an expression of love and fidelity to God rather than simply fulfilling duty. In Matthew 22:37–39, Jesus emphasizes love of God and neighbor as the greatest commandments. Obedience rooted in relationship cultivates the heart and aligns human behavior with the Eternal's intentions.

Christ models moral perfection and relational guidance not by coercion but through example. His interactions with disciples, the marginalized, and those in need reveal a pattern of life in alignment with divine order. In Luke 19:10, it is stated, "For the Son of Man came to seek and to save the lost." Each act embodies mercy, justice, and compassion, showing that ethical living is inseparable from relational engagement with God. Human hearts, attuned to the light of Christ, learn to perceive the moral texture of reality in a relational context.

The relational dimension of God's presence transforms human understanding of moral and spiritual life. Where shadows of the Eternal previously offered glimpses through dharma or satya, the incarnation demonstrates fullness. Ethical insights become encounters with a personal guide who speaks, listens, and accompanies. The practice of virtues shifts from abstract exercise to lived participation in the divine life. Prayer, contemplation, and obedience are now channels for experiencing the intimate reality of God's care and guidance.

In this relational encounter, ethical, moral, and spiritual shadows are no longer isolated ideals. They are integrated into a living friendship with Christ, who embodies love, wisdom, and relational attentiveness. Human longing for completeness finds satisfaction as hearts respond with trust, imitation of Christ's example, and active engagement in moral and spiritual formation. The Eternal Word entering history illuminates the path for human life, showing that true ethical and spiritual fulfillment emerges within the context of personal relationship with God.

6.4 Ethical and Spiritual Formation in the Word Made Flesh

The life of Christ offers a tangible model for ethical and spiritual formation. As the Eternal Word made flesh, Jesus embodies the principles of truth, mercy, and righteousness in concrete, relatable ways. His teachings are not abstract precepts but invitations to participate in a life shaped by divine wisdom. In the Sermon on the Mount, Jesus calls his followers to a higher understanding of moral life, teaching that anger, lust, and vengeance are not merely external wrongs but conditions of the heart that require transformation. In Matthew 5:6, he says, "Blessed are those who hunger and thirst for righteousness, for they will be filled." This emphasis on internal disposition highlights the alignment of conscience with divine intention.

Christ's engagement with the human heart connects deeply to the inner moral awareness discussed in previous chapters. Where conscience and dharmic principles previously offered guidance through intuition and reflection, the Word made flesh clarifies and deepens these insights. Human discernment, once partial and shadowed, now encounters fullness in Christ's teachings, miracles, and relational guidance. Parables such as the Good Samaritan (Luke 10:25–37) reveal that ethical formation is inseparable from love and relational responsibility. Moral knowledge becomes active and lived, shaping not only thought but behavior, attitude, and priorities.

Responding to Christ initiates profound human transformation. Virtues like compassion, patience, and integrity move from being ideals to practiced realities. Acts of mercy, generosity, and forgiveness emerge as natural expressions of a heart aligned with the eternal order. Spiritual formation unfolds through participation in the life of Christ, whether in prayer, communal worship, or service to others. The human heart is reshaped, no longer guided by shadows of moral truth alone, but by the presence of the Word who embodies and enlivens that truth.

Ethical and spiritual formation in the Word made flesh is therefore relational, experiential, and transformative. The human response is not only obedience but a cultivation of character that mirrors divine qualities. Conscience, once a faint guide, becomes illuminated by Christ's example and instruction. Daily life transforms into a field where moral and spiritual growth is nurtured, and virtues previously glimpsed in ethical traditions now take root and flourish. Through Christ, the Eternal Word integrates moral insight, relational engagement, and spiritual depth into the lived human experience.

6.5 Light and Word in Human Experience

Human experience is full of moments where the Word and Light intersect with daily life, revealing the presence of God in tangible ways. Prayer provides one of the most immediate avenues for encountering the Eternal. In the act of lifting the mind and heart in dialogue with God, the Word becomes alive, shaping thought and guiding conscience. In Scripture reading, the words of Christ are not merely historical text but living instruction that illuminates decisions, relationships, and inner moral discernment. As Psalm

119:105 affirms, "Your word is a lamp to my feet and a light to my path," indicating the guiding power of divine speech in everyday life.

Worship is another context where human perception of the Eternal is deepened. Singing, silence, and communal participation awaken the heart to the moral and spiritual dimensions of life. In the sacraments, ordinary elements such as bread, wine, water, and oil become channels of grace, pointing beyond themselves to the presence of Christ. These experiences allow the faithful to encounter the Word not as abstract philosophy but as personal, active, and transformative. Human perception is sharpened, and what once seemed mundane reveals layers of ethical and spiritual significance.

Christ's teaching consistently demonstrates how the Light penetrates human darkness. Parables such as the lost sheep and the prodigal son (Luke 15) offer insight into moral realities while simultaneously illustrating relational care. Ordinary acts of mercy, patience, and truth are illuminated by the relational Word, showing how divine guidance operates in real-life situations. The moral intuition discussed in previous chapters, previously an echo of higher law, now finds clarity and purpose in the lived presence of Christ.

In reflecting on these encounters, the resonance between Vedic insights and the Christian revelation becomes apparent. The concept of Jyoti, the inner light revealing truth, and the moral intuition that guides conscience, find fulfillment in the relational presence of Christ. Every ordinary moment can become a point of illumination, where light and Word converge, shaping understanding, guiding action, and nurturing the human heart toward deeper communion with the Eternal.

6.6 Fulfillment of the Shadows

The ethical, moral, and spiritual ideals explored in Chapter 4—dharma, satya, ahimsa, and the cultivation of virtues—serve as glimpses of the Eternal, hinting at a reality beyond human comprehension. These shadows point toward the heart's longing for goodness, truth, and relational love. While they guide conscience and inspire ethical living, they are ultimately incomplete. They prepare the human heart for the fullness of divine presence, yet they cannot themselves satisfy the deep yearning for relational communion with God.

Christ enters this narrative as the embodiment of these ideals, perfecting what moral intuition and ethical reflection can only approximate. In his life and teaching, love is not an abstract concept but a lived reality. Justice is not merely a social ideal but an expression of divine righteousness. Mercy becomes tangible through acts of healing, forgiveness, and compassion. For example, the parable of the Good Samaritan in Luke 10:25–37 illustrates the relational dimension of justice and care, showing how moral duty extends beyond rigid rules into personal engagement and heartfelt action.

Satya, the pursuit of ultimate truth, finds its completion in Christ as the Word incarnate. Truth is no longer a distant concept to be discerned through reflection alone; it is a living presence who speaks, teaches, and calls humanity into alignment with divine reality. Similarly, the practice of ahimsa, the reverence for life, finds its ultimate expression in Christ's self-giving love, which demonstrates the fullest respect for human dignity and the sacredness of life.

The relational dimension of fulfillment is especially evident in Christ's interactions. By calling disciples, forgiving sinners, and embracing the marginalized, he transforms abstract ethical principles into lived relationships marked by mercy, trust, and love. Human hearts experience moral ideals as personal invitations to participate in the divine life. The shadows of dharma, satya, and ahimsa no longer remain distant; they are made concrete and accessible in the person of Christ, revealing the Eternal not as an abstract standard but as an intimate, guiding presence in human life.

6.7 The Word as Life-Giving

In the incarnation, the Word not only reveals truth and perfects moral ideals but also brings life in its fullest sense. The life that Christ offers is both spiritual and practical, touching every dimension of human existence. Spiritual transformation begins as the heart responds to his presence with faith and openness, allowing the light of the Word to illuminate areas of doubt, fear, and moral confusion. This illumination is not merely intellectual but deeply personal, awakening hope, courage, and a renewed sense of purpose.

Moral courage emerges as one experiences the life-giving Word. The example of Christ's obedience to the Father, even unto suffering, calls followers to act justly and love generously in the face of societal pressures and personal challenges. In John 10:10, Jesus speaks of giving life in abundance, highlighting that participation in his life is not passive but transformative, encouraging ethical engagement and relational depth.

Human response to this gift of life is multifaceted. Faith invites trust in the promises of God and reliance on divine guidance.

Obedience expresses alignment of the heart and will with the Eternal. Love manifests relationally, both toward God and toward neighbors. Participation in divine life becomes the fulfillment of the longings the human heart has sensed in moral shadows, intuitive conscience, and glimpses of truth. Life in Christ unites spiritual awakening, ethical living, and relational intimacy into a coherent experience of the Eternal made tangible in history.

Conclusion: Encountering the Eternal in Person

The journey from moral shadows and ethical glimpses to the fullness of relational encounter reaches its culmination in Christ. Where once the heart sensed goodness, truth, and beauty through dharma, satya, and ahimsa, it now meets the Eternal in a personal, living presence. In the Gospel of John, the Word is revealed as both light and life, drawing humanity into an intimate relationship that transforms understanding, moral discernment, and daily living.

This encounter is not abstract or distant. The Eternal engages the human heart directly, calling for trust, love, and responsiveness. The ideals glimpsed in creation, conscience, and cultural wisdom are no longer mere reflections or shadows. They are fulfilled in the life, teachings, and presence of Christ, who embodies truth, mercy, justice, and relational love. Each moment of prayer, reflection, and ethical action becomes an opportunity to perceive the Word speaking in and through everyday life.

Reflective questions guide the reader to personal application. How does Christ illuminate the virtues, ethical insights, and moral intuitions you have encountered in your life? In what ways does the Word call you to respond, to align your choices and relationships with the eternal truths now revealed in history? These questions invite an ongoing, living engagement with the Eternal, encouraging readers to experience the Word not as an idea but as a companion, guide, and source of life.

Chapter 7: Life, Light, and Love

Human hearts have an innate longing that reaches beyond ordinary existence. From the earliest moments of awareness, people sense that life is more than the daily routine, that understanding is more than mere information, and that love is meant to be experienced deeply and reciprocally. These longings were explored in earlier chapters through the moral and ethical ideals of dharma, satya, and ahimsa, as well as through the glimpses of divine care in Krishna's actions. Yet these shadows and reflections point to something more, something that satisfies the heart fully and personally.

Christ enters this picture as the one who embodies life, light, and love in ways that human imagination alone could never achieve. In the Gospel of John, he is described as the Word who became flesh and dwelt among us, full of grace and truth. His presence fulfills the desires that ethical ideals and spiritual intuition have only hinted at. In him, life is not simply existence; it is abundant, transformative, and eternal. The light he brings does not merely illuminate knowledge or insight but guides moral discernment and awakens the conscience. His love is active, relational, and transformative, inviting human hearts into participation rather than imposing obligation.

Encountering Christ challenges us to recognize that our deepest longings—whether for protection, guidance, forgiveness, or unconditional love—are oriented toward a personal and relational reality. Human hearts do not yearn in vain; they are attuned to the Eternal who meets these desires in historical, tangible ways. Reflection invites each person to ask: How does Christ meet the deepest needs of my heart? In what ways is life renewed, understanding clarified, and love expressed in my daily encounters? These questions prepare us to perceive the richness of life, light, and love that flows through the Word made flesh, setting the stage for the unfolding journey in this chapter.

7.1: Life in Christ – Beyond Mere Existence

Life in Christ offers a depth and fullness that surpasses mere survival or the accumulation of material goods. In the Gospel of John, Jesus speaks of coming that his followers may have life and have it abundantly, inviting human hearts into a reality where existence is rich with purpose, meaning, and relational depth. This abundance is not measured by wealth, status, or earthly comfort, but by the vitality of one's inner life, the growth of the conscience, and the flourishing of moral courage in daily choices.

Ordinary life, without engagement with the Eternal, often drifts through cycles of routine and superficial satisfactions. Joy and purpose may appear momentarily, yet the human spirit senses incompleteness. In contrast, life in Christ integrates the physical, emotional, and spiritual dimensions of existence. Trust in him nurtures hope that does not fade under pressure. Engagement with his teachings cultivates discernment and ethical clarity, guiding individuals to act rightly even when faced with difficult circumstances. The heart that opens to Christ experiences renewal, not as a distant promise but as a present transformation, where love, mercy, and moral awareness grow hand in hand with faith.

Human experience testifies to this transformation in subtle and profound ways. People who encounter Christ often report a renewed capacity to forgive, to persevere through suffering, and to act with compassion toward others. The abundant life Jesus offers does not eliminate challenges, yet it empowers the individual to navigate them with courage and trust. In this way, life in Christ becomes more than existence; it is a flourishing, relational, and moral journey, inviting each person to participate fully in the eternal reality he embodies.

7.2 Light of Understanding and Moral Discernment

The presence of Christ brings illumination that transforms human understanding and moral perception. In the Gospel of John, he identifies himself as the light of the world, revealing not only spiritual truth but also the path by which human hearts may navigate ethical choices. This light is relational, reaching into the life of each individual and offering clarity where confusion, doubt, or moral uncertainty might otherwise prevail. It is both a guidance and a presence, showing the way toward righteous action and deeper insight into God's intentions for humanity.

Christ's light fulfills what was hinted at in earlier reflections on inner illumination. In Chapter 2, we explored the concept of inner light, Jyoti, as the awakening of insight and discernment. In the historical life of Jesus, this light becomes tangible and personal. His interactions with disciples reveal this clearly: he interprets the Law and the prophets with authority, clarifies the meaning of parables, and illuminates the heart's intentions in ways that foster understanding and ethical maturity. Encounters with seekers, whether in teaching, healing, or conversation, demonstrate that this illumination is not abstract but enacted relationally, guiding both thought and action toward what is true and good.

The human response to this light involves attentiveness, humility, and willingness to be shaped. As the light penetrates the mind and conscience, it calls individuals to recognize moral truths they might have sensed dimly and to act in accordance with them. Through Christ, the promises of insight and guidance become accessible in history, allowing the moral and spiritual longings explored in previous chapters to find relational fulfillment and practical application in everyday life.

7.3 Love as the Core of Divine Action

The love of Christ stands at the heart of all divine action, offering a model that is both personal and transformative. In John 13:34–35, he commands his followers to love one another as he has loved them, establishing love as the defining mark of discipleship. This love is not abstract; it engages the entire person, shaping thought, action, and relationships. It addresses the deep longings of the human heart for connection, justice, and care, echoing the shadows of dharma, satya, and ahimsa discussed in Chapters 4 and 5. Through Christ, these ethical and moral aspirations are fulfilled in a relational and living form.

Human experience of this love occurs in both ordinary and profound ways. Acts of kindness, forgiveness, and empathy become reflections of the divine, allowing believers to embody the transformative love they have received. This relational love guides ethical decision-making, cultivates patience, and fosters reconciliation in community. The encounter with Christ's love is both formative and participatory: it teaches the heart to respond rightly, to extend mercy, and to live in harmony with God's will. Through receiving and reflecting this love, individuals discover the fulfillment of moral and spiritual yearnings, experiencing a relational connection that engages both conscience and heart.

7.4 Integration – Life, Light, and Love in Daily Living

In daily living, life, light, and love converge in ways that shape both spiritual awareness and practical action. Life in Christ offers hope and renewal, transforming ordinary existence into a journey with purpose and meaning, as emphasized in John 10:10. Light provides guidance, revealing truth and clarifying moral and ethical decisions, reflecting the illumination Christ brings to human understanding as seen in passages such as John 8:12. Love serves as the motivating force, guiding choices, deepening relationships, and

forming character according to the example of Christ's command to love one another.
Scripture offers numerous illustrations of this integration in human experience. In Luke 19:1–10, the encounter of Zacchaeus with Christ shows life renewed through relational engagement, light revealed through understanding of personal shortcomings, and love expressed in restitution and transformation. Everyday experiences reflect similar patterns: choosing compassion over self-interest, speaking truth with integrity, and acting with kindness mirrors the presence of Christ in ordinary circumstances. Observing conscience, responding to moral intuition, and extending care to others become tangible ways of participating in the life, light, and love Christ provides, demonstrating that spiritual principles are inseparable from the lived realities of human existence.

Conclusion: Encountering the Reality the Heart Seeks
Encountering Christ is not an abstract exercise but a tangible reality that engages the whole heart. He is present in everyday decisions, in moments of reflection, in the ethical and moral choices that shape our lives, and in the love we extend to others. Life flows through those who trust in him, offering hope and renewal that transcends circumstances. Light illuminates understanding, providing clarity in confusion and guidance in moral complexity. Love shapes relationships, teaching patience, empathy, and selflessness, reflecting the relational character of God revealed in Christ.

Consider these questions: Where is life evident in your daily choices and actions? In what ways does light guide your understanding of truth and morality? How is love influencing your relationships and decisions? These reflections invite continued awareness of Christ's presence, encouraging active participation in the fullness of life, illumination, and love that he embodies. The heart's search finds its fulfillment not only in recognizing these truths but in living them, moment by moment, in communion with the One who makes all things new.

Chapter 8: The Response of the Heart

The human heart carries an innate capacity to recognize and respond to what is true, good, and beautiful. From the earliest stirrings of conscience to the subtle yearnings for justice, love, and mercy, there is within each person a natural orientation toward what is beyond themselves. When the longings explored in earlier chapters intersect with moments of moral awareness or glimpses of divine presence, the heart is awakened to a response that is both personal and free. This awakening is not forced or imposed; it is an invitation extended by the Eternal, patiently waiting for the human spirit to turn and engage.

Reflection and attentiveness are among the first movements of this response. Observing the world, considering moral choices, or noticing the inner stirrings of empathy can open pathways to recognizing God's presence. The Scriptures depict such openness as central to a life of faith. In the Gospel of John, Jesus calls his followers into relationship, not as a demand but as a revelation of love and guidance, showing that genuine response begins with recognition and openness to the Word made flesh. Similarly, the Psalms repeatedly invite hearts to attend, listen, and incline toward God, highlighting that responsiveness is as much about posture and attention as it is about intellect or ritual.

The forms this response takes vary widely across human experience. Some may sense it through contemplative prayer, where silence allows the heart to hear the subtle promptings of God. Others experience it through acts of ethical discernment, where conscience, informed by virtue and intuition, directs one toward right action. These responses are not merely functional; they are relational. Trust, gratitude, and the desire to align with what is true emerge naturally when the heart recognizes the goodness and faithfulness of the Divine.

As readers reflect on their own lives, questions arise: How does my heart recognize the presence of God in ordinary moments? In what ways am I attentive to the moral intuitions, relationships, and inner stirrings that may be invitations to engage more fully with the Eternal? Is my response shaped by fear, obligation, or by a free movement toward love and understanding? These inquiries highlight the delicate interplay between divine invitation and human freedom.

The heart is capable of responding, but it is awakened only when longing, reflection, and openness converge.

This awakening marks the beginning of a journey rather than its conclusion. It prepares the individual to engage relationally with the Word, to participate in the life, light, and love that Christ offers, and to translate spiritual awareness into ethical living. It is within this space of attentive readiness that the human response takes root, signaling the start of a path where moral insight, relational trust, and personal reflection converge into an authentic encounter with the Divine.

8.1 Reflection and Awareness

Human beings are naturally equipped to notice subtle movements of awareness, moments when the ordinary becomes infused with deeper significance. Attentive reflection is the practice of slowing down and listening to these stirrings of the heart. It is in these quiet spaces, whether while walking through a forest, pausing to consider a moral decision, or simply sitting in contemplation, that the presence of God can be sensed. The Vedic concept of inner hearing, or śruti, underscores the importance of attunement to subtle truths, suggesting that awareness is not merely an intellectual exercise but a spiritual practice that shapes perception and moral sensibility.

Ethical decision-making provides another arena for reflection. When faced with choices that challenge conscience, the heart becomes aware of guidance beyond mere rules. The recognition that some actions align with goodness while others diminish life reveals an intuitive awareness of a moral order. Human conscience resonates with these truths, echoing earlier reflections on dharma, satya, and ahimsa as glimpses of an eternal standard. These experiences remind individuals that attention to daily life, relationships, and ethical obligations forms a channel through which the Eternal communicates.

Moments of awe and wonder further cultivate reflective awareness. Observing the sunrise, listening to a river's flow, or contemplating the vastness of the night sky can evoke a profound sense of connection and humility. These instances awaken the heart to the presence of life, light, and relational depth that transcends immediate circumstances. In this, reflection is inseparable from moral and spiritual awakening, creating an integrated response that engages mind, heart, and soul.

Personal introspection completes the cycle of reflection. Considering one's motives, emotions, and longings provides insight into how the heart responds to God's call. As Christ models relational engagement and moral clarity, the human response becomes both conscious and relational. Awareness is thus an active posture, where observation, ethical attention, and inner listening converge, inviting the heart to respond freely to the presence it senses and values.

8.2 Trust and Openness

Trust is a fundamental expression of the human heart responding to the Divine. It emerges not as an obligation or an abstract principle but as a reliance on God's guidance, love, and providence. Trust involves the willingness to allow one's life to be oriented toward a source beyond oneself, recognizing that ultimate wisdom and care surpass human understanding. In the Gospels, disciples often exemplify this trust, following Christ even when the path is uncertain. When Peter steps out of the boat toward Jesus in Matthew 14:28–31, the act reflects not just courage but a relational confidence that Christ sustains and leads.

Human experience mirrors this same dynamic. In moments of suffering, confusion, or moral ambiguity, individuals often encounter the call to place trust in something beyond immediate perception. Trust in God is revealed in the small decisions of everyday life: choosing honesty when deception would be easier, extending forgiveness when resentment is easier to harbor, and seeking guidance when answers are not apparent. These acts demonstrate that trust is cultivated through relational awareness, through attentiveness to the presence and action of God in ordinary circumstances.

Openness accompanies trust. A heart cannot rely on God if it resists engagement or clings solely to self-sufficiency. Openness involves listening, observing, and responding with willingness, mirroring the relational patterns Christ models in his interactions. The Samaritan woman at the well in John 4 exemplifies openness when she allows conversation and encounter to transform her understanding and relationships. Here, trust and openness are inseparable, forming a natural human response that honors the relational and personal nature of God.

In practice, trust and openness nurture spiritual resilience. They foster a capacity to navigate uncertainty, moral tension, and ethical responsibility with courage and hope. Human hearts learn to recognize that divine guidance is not coercive but invitational, and that relational engagement offers both moral clarity and emotional grounding. Through trust and openness, the human response becomes a living dialogue, a participation in the ongoing presence of God in the midst of life.

8.3 Relationship and Communion

Relationship with God is the natural unfolding of trust and openness, moving the heart from awareness into communion. Prayer becomes the language of this engagement, not as a rigid formula but as genuine conversation with the Eternal. Worship provides a space where human attention aligns with divine presence, and reflection on God's actions fosters moral alignment and ethical responsiveness. In this relational framework, the heart experiences the fulfillment of longings previously glimpsed through conscience, moral ideals, and shadows of the Eternal.

Human life offers countless illustrations of relational response. Acts of care toward family, friends, and even strangers reflect the participation in God's sustaining love. Forgiveness in situations of conflict mirrors the mercy experienced through Christ, while service to those in need becomes an enactment of divine justice and compassion. Each act of moral engagement, when rooted in attention to God's presence, deepens the relational bond and cultivates a lived experience of communion.

The continuity from longing to fulfillment is evident in the trajectory of human experience. Chapter 5 explored the deep yearning for salvation and righteousness, while Chapters 6 and 7 highlighted Christ as the embodiment of life, light, and love. Now, relational engagement allows that embodiment to transform daily living. Through prayer, reflection, ethical action, and worship, human hearts actively participate in the reality of God's presence. This relational response does not require perfection but invites ongoing attentiveness and responsiveness, forming a rhythm of life where the Eternal is known through intimate encounter and sustained practice.

Communion with God reshapes perception and action, reinforcing the moral, spiritual, and emotional dimensions of human life. By recognizing divine presence in ordinary experiences and acting in alignment with love, truth, and service, individuals participate in the relational life for which they were created. The response of the heart thus becomes both natural and transformative, bridging longing and fulfillment into living engagement with the Eternal.

8.4 Transformation Through Response

Transformation through response is the natural fruit of a heart that actively engages with the Divine. When reflection deepens, the mind becomes aware of patterns of thought, desire, and intention, allowing ethical discernment to take root. Trust nurtures courage to act in alignment with moral insight, while relational openness creates space for love, patience, and humility to flourish. This combination reshapes character gradually, not through coercion, but through attentive participation in God's presence.

Human experience illustrates this transformative process in tangible ways. Acts of empathy toward those in suffering, the cultivation of patience in difficult relationships, and the willingness to forgive mirror internal growth prompted by attentive responsiveness to the Divine. Moments of moral struggle and decision-making become opportunities for conscience to be refined. As the heart engages relationally with God, ethical intuition is strengthened, and resilience emerges in facing challenges, disappointment, or injustice.

Relational formation occurs as the heart matures through repeated responses to divine invitation. The individual learns to align personal desires with higher truths, integrating moral awareness with emotional sensitivity and spiritual insight. Character is not molded in isolation but through ongoing interaction with God's guidance, light, and love. Each instance of attentive reflection, trust, and moral action contributes to the cultivation of a life increasingly shaped by virtue, insight, and relational harmony. In this way, the response of the heart leads to a holistic transformation, drawing the whole person into the life for which they were created.

Conclusion: Living the Response of the Heart

Responding to God is not a singular act but a lifelong journey of attentive reflection, trust, and relational engagement. The heart grows in awareness when one pauses to notice the gentle guidance, moral prompting, and sustaining presence of God in daily life. Reflection allows the mind to recognize moments of insight and ethical clarity. Trust encourages the individual to rely on divine wisdom and love, even when circumstances are uncertain or challenging. Relational openness cultivates a willingness to receive guidance, offer forgiveness, and extend care to others, reflecting the relational nature of God.

Consider your own life: how do you notice God's presence in your thoughts, decisions, and interactions? In what ways are you learning to trust more deeply, to listen more attentively, and to act in alignment with love and truth? Each moment of attentiveness and each choice to respond shapes the heart and fosters spiritual growth. Participation in the life, light, and love of Christ is an invitation, not an obligation. The Divine waits with patience and care, inviting personal encounter at each stage of the journey. Engaging with this invitation nurtures a heart that is attuned to God, capable of ethical discernment, and open to the transformative power of relational love.

Part IV — Glimpses in Hindu Scriptures

Throughout history, divine truth has never remained hidden from the seeking heart. The Eternal has allowed every culture to perceive fragments of light that awaken the soul to His presence. In the sacred literature of India, this illumination appears in poetic hymns, philosophical dialogues, and profound reflections on life and divinity. These writings reveal that the human spirit has always reached upward toward the unseen, longing to understand the source of creation and the meaning of existence.

Part IV of this work examines these ancient texts with deep reverence and discernment. The author approaches them not as parallel revelations but as witnesses of humanity's spiritual intuition. The hymns of the Vedas, the meditations of the Upanishads, and the moral insights of later scriptures reveal the human desire to know the Supreme Reality. Within their poetic language appear glimpses of eternal principles—truth, holiness, sacrifice, and devotion—that reflect the divine image within humanity.

Each chapter in this section invites the reader to listen carefully to these ancient voices. Their expressions of longing for purity, liberation, and divine communion arise from the same awareness that all creation depends upon a transcendent source. The Vedic vision of the cosmic order, the Upanishadic search for the ultimate Self, and the devotional yearning of later traditions all point toward a divine reality that transcends human limitation. These glimpses of spiritual light show that God has been preparing hearts through ages to receive the fullness of His revelation.

The author highlights passages that resonate with timeless truths already revealed in Scripture. The themes of divine creation, moral order, and spiritual awakening found in these texts serve as bridges of understanding, guiding the mind from intuition toward revelation. Through such exploration, the reader learns how divine grace works through history and culture, gently leading seekers toward the true knowledge of God.

Part IV, therefore, becomes a study in both reverence and revelation. It honors the depth of India's sacred tradition while showing that every authentic longing for truth finds completion in the living Word. These glimpses are like rays of the morning sun that announce the coming of full day.

Chapter 9: Glimpses of the Eternal in Hindu Scriptures

Human hearts carry a natural longing that transcends circumstances, culture, and time. Across civilizations, people have sought truth, goodness, and love as realities that reach beyond the fleeting concerns of daily life. Within Hindu scriptures, this yearning finds expression in multiple ways. The Rig Veda often reflects a sense of awe and reverence for forces larger than oneself, suggesting that human beings sense something eternal even when it is not fully revealed. The Upanishads guide seekers toward introspection and moral awareness, encouraging reflection on the nature of self and the ultimate reality, Brahman. The Bhagavad Gita, in particular, portrays a relational understanding of duty and righteousness, where ethical action is not merely obedience but participation in a larger moral and spiritual order. Bhakti literature, including the hymns of Mirabai and Tulsidas, gives voice to longing for intimacy, surrender, and divine love, showing how devotion awakens the heart to the Divine in personal ways.

These texts, while diverse in expression, converge in pointing beyond themselves toward something greater. Ethical precepts such as dharma and satya cultivate awareness of right action and moral responsibility, while devotional practice fosters longing and trust toward a reality that is at once relational and transcendent. Philosophical inquiry and meditation illuminate human capacity for introspection and ethical discernment. Readers encountering these traditions can see that Hindu scriptures often present partial but profound glimpses of what the human heart seeks: a moral anchor, relational care, and ultimate goodness.

Reflection questions arise naturally from these observations. How does engagement with ethical ideals cultivate attentiveness and responsiveness in your own life? What patterns of longing, love, and devotion in the texts resonate with your own moral and spiritual intuition? In what ways do philosophical insights invite a deeper awareness of the Divine within and around you? These questions invite careful contemplation, opening the heart to recognize the movements of the eternal even when the fullness of God has not yet been revealed.

9.1 Ethical Ideals as Shadows of God

In Hindu scriptures, ethical ideals function as subtle guides that point toward a higher moral and spiritual reality. Dharma, often understood as righteous duty or moral order, provides a framework for individuals to act with responsibility and care toward others. Following dharma encourages reflection on the consequences of one's actions, fostering an inner awareness that aligns personal choices with the well-being of the community. Satya, or truthfulness, directs attention not only to honesty in speech and action but also to alignment with a deeper moral reality, suggesting that truth itself carries a transcendent significance beyond immediate human concerns. Ahimsa, the principle of non-violence, cultivates sensitivity and empathy, shaping how individuals relate to all forms of life and promoting ethical discernment in everyday encounters.

Other virtues highlighted in the texts, such as compassion, patience, forgiveness, and self-control, act as formative practices that strengthen character and conscience. When individuals practice these virtues, they refine moral awareness and cultivate relational sensitivity, allowing them to respond with justice, care, and understanding in complex situations. Historical and contemporary examples illustrate these ideals in action: a person choosing honesty despite social pressure, offering aid to those in need, or demonstrating restraint and empathy in moments of conflict. The ethical patterns embedded in Hindu teachings do more than prescribe behavior; they awaken the heart to recognize a standard of goodness that points beyond the human self toward the Eternal.

Engaging with these principles prompts reflective questions: How do moments of moral choice reveal the deeper patterns of right action in your own life? In what ways does striving for justice and compassion align your conscience with something beyond ordinary human understanding? How do practices like honesty, care, and restraint shape your relationships and cultivate ethical awareness? Observing these shadows of God in ethical living opens the human heart to perceive the presence of the Divine, even when the fullness of revelation remains unseen.

9.2 Devotional Longing and Bhakti

In the Bhakti tradition of Hinduism, the human heart is portrayed as naturally inclined toward love, devotion, and surrender to the Divine. Texts such as the Bhagavata Purana and the works of Alvars and other devotional poets emphasize a yearning for intimate relationship with God, where love and surrender become central expressions of spiritual life. This devotional longing is not merely ritualistic or intellectual but arises from a deep recognition that the heart's desires cannot be fully satisfied by material pursuits alone. The devotee seeks protection, guidance, and presence from a personal God who is both near and transcendent.

Bhakti practices such as prayer, singing hymns, meditation on the divine form, and acts of service cultivate a relational awareness in which the devotee experiences God's presence in daily life. Stories of devotees like Prahlada and Mirabai illustrate how love and trust in God provide courage and hope even amid difficulty and danger. The human longing expressed in these texts resonates with an intuitive sense that the heart is designed for connection with a higher personal reality. In this context, devotion becomes a language of the soul, a means of aligning ethical living, moral awareness, and emotional desire toward the Eternal.

Reflective questions arise from engaging with these devotional texts: How does your own sense of longing for love and guidance point beyond what the material world can provide? In what ways does surrender, trust, and devotion cultivate intimacy with the Divine in daily life? Observing the intensity and sincerity of Bhakti devotion offers insight into the natural human orientation toward relational fulfillment and prepares the heart to recognize the fullness of God's presence when revealed.

9.3 Philosophical Glimpses of the Eternal

In the Upanishads, human reflection on ultimate reality encourages the heart to reach beyond immediate experience and consider the nature of being itself. The concepts of Brahman as the unchanging, infinite reality and atman as the innermost self prompt individuals to examine the moral and spiritual dimensions of their lives. Texts such as the Chandogya Upanishad and the Brihadaranyaka Upanishad illustrate that understanding the self's connection with the ultimate is inseparable from cultivating ethical awareness, compassion, and disciplined living. By contemplating the harmony and order of the cosmos, the seeker develops a sensitivity to both moral responsibility and relational meaning, realizing that personal conduct reflects participation in a larger, intelligible order.

The Upanishadic emphasis on knowledge as a path to liberation encourages introspection and self-examination without insisting on rigid formulas or dogmatic claims. Ethical life, self-discipline, and attentiveness to truth naturally arise as one reflects on the unity of atman and Brahman, fostering a readiness to respond to the Divine relationally. In this way, intellectual engagement functions as preparation for a more personal encounter with God, cultivating discernment, humility, and openness. Reflective questions emerge from this process: How does understanding the interconnectedness of life and the self guide your moral choices? In what ways does contemplation of ultimate reality awaken a sense of relational responsibility and inner longing for the Eternal? The philosophical insights of the Upanishads awaken the heart and mind, forming a bridge between ethical awareness and the fullness of relational knowledge that is revealed in God's Word.

9.4 Limitations and Preparation for Fulfillment

Hindu scriptures provide profound moral and spiritual insights, yet they often offer glimpses rather than complete fulfillment of the human heart's yearning for a personal and relational God. The ethical guidance of dharma, the pursuit of truth in satya, and the cultivation of compassion through ahimsa present patterns of moral life that awaken conscience and ethical sensitivity. Devotional practices in the Bhakti tradition stir longing for intimacy with the Divine, and philosophical reflection in the Upanishads encourages self-examination and awareness of ultimate reality. Each of these elements acts as a preparation, forming a receptive heart without fully satisfying the innate desire for relational encounter with God.

Human experience mirrors this partial fulfillment. Moments of repentance, ethical striving, or heartfelt prayer can evoke a sense of encountering something beyond oneself, stirring longing for completeness and communion. Individuals recognize the limitations of ethical ideals alone, experiencing that moral living and intellectual reflection, while essential, do not fully answer the human craving for love, forgiveness, and relational guidance. These shadows of divine life prepare the heart to recognize Christ, who embodies and perfects the virtues, relational intimacy, and moral guidance hinted at in Hindu texts. Reflective questions arise: How have your moral efforts or devotional practices stirred a deeper longing? In what ways do experiences of ethical striving or spiritual insight point toward the need for a personal, living God? Awareness of these limitations becomes a gateway for openness to Christ, whose life and teaching fulfill the ethical, spiritual, and relational yearnings awakened in the human heart.

Conclusion: From Shadows to Fullness

Hindu scriptures provide moral, devotional, and philosophical guidance that awakens the human heart to higher truths and ethical living. Through the practice of dharma, pursuit of satya, cultivation of ahimsa, devotional surrender, and reflection on Brahman and atman, individuals are invited to recognize patterns of goodness, love, and ultimate reality. These glimpses act as shadows, illuminating the innate human desire for a personal and relational God, yet they do not fully satisfy the heart's deepest longings.

Reflective questions invite engagement: Which ethical ideals or spiritual practices have stirred a deeper yearning within you? How have moments of devotional surrender or philosophical insight guided your awareness toward a fuller relationship with the Divine? Awareness of these partial insights nurtures openness, anticipation, and receptivity. The human heart, stirred by moral striving and devotional longing, is prepared to encounter the fullness of God's presence. This preparation bridges naturally toward the Word made flesh, who enters history to complete and perfect what these glimpses have anticipated, as explored in the following chapters on Christ's relational and transformative work in human life.

Part V — Living in the Light

As we move into the final section of this work, *Living in the Light* invites readers to enter the practical and transformative dimension of spiritual truth. The preceding sections have explored the depths of revelation, the reflections across world religions, and the fullness of understanding found in Christ. Now, the focus shifts from knowing and discerning truth to embodying it in daily life. This part is not merely theoretical; it is a guide for integrating spiritual insights into every thought, decision, and action.

Living in the light is more than moral correctness or ritual observance—it is a dynamic, ongoing experience of God's presence, illuminating the path of life with clarity, courage, and compassion. It addresses the subtle tensions between human frailty and divine guidance, showing how faith is lived moment by moment. The chapters here highlight practical wisdom, spiritual disciplines, and the cultivation of character, emphasizing that the journey of light is both inward and outward: shaping the heart while impacting the world.

Readers will encounter reflections on vigilance, discernment, and perseverance, alongside encouragement to cultivate habits that sustain spiritual growth. Each chapter demonstrates how light functions as both a metaphor and a reality: a source of direction in confusion, a purifier in the midst of moral compromise, and a comfort in times of uncertainty. By exploring these dimensions, this section encourages believers to embrace a life that is transparent before God and beneficial to others.

Ultimately, *Living in the Light* is an invitation to walk in harmony with divine truth, allowing the illumination of God's presence to transform ordinary routines into sacred practices. It challenges readers to move from passive understanding to active participation, fostering a life that radiates integrity, hope, and love. As the culmination of this journey, this section bridges knowledge and action, inspiring a faith that is vibrant, enduring, and fully lived.

Chapter 10: Satyam, Shivam, Christam- Eternal Harmony

Human beings carry within them an innate longing to encounter what is ultimate, enduring, and true. This longing manifests in the pursuit of knowledge, moral clarity, and relationships that transcend self-interest. Across cultures and eras, hearts have sought reality that can be trusted, goodness that can guide action, and love that satisfies the deepest desire for connection. The human spirit does not rest with fleeting experiences of pleasure, power, or material achievement. Even in ordinary moments, people feel an echo of something greater—a call toward a truth that is constant, a goodness that transforms, and a love that redeems.

The concept of Satyam, or eternal truth, reflects this pursuit. It is not merely intellectual knowledge but a recognition of what is real and reliable, that which aligns with the moral and cosmic order. Ancient texts such as the Upanishads describe Brahman as the ultimate reality, the foundation from which all understanding flows. Human conscience, the inner faculty discerning right from wrong, participates in this recognition. When a person senses integrity, honesty, or ethical coherence, they are touching a fragment of eternal truth that transcends cultural and temporal boundaries.

Closely related is Shivam, the principle of moral goodness and virtue. Ethics, compassion, self-restraint, and justice are not arbitrary rules but glimpses of a moral order rooted in the Divine. Hindu texts such as the Bhagavad Gita describe dharma as a guiding principle that sustains life and society, reflecting the character of the eternal. In daily experience, when one chooses to act with care, courage, and integrity, the heart encounters a dimension of goodness that points beyond itself toward the Divine.

The triad finds its culmination in Christam, Jesus Christ as the fullness of truth, moral goodness, and relational love. In the Gospel of John, the Logos is described as both the source of creation and the living Word dwelling among humanity, embodying what the heart has sought in fragments through conscience, ethical striving, and relational desire. Christ reveals the perfect integration of truth and goodness and extends love personally to each individual. This triadic framework is not a static concept but an invitation for the human heart to awaken, recognize, and engage with the Divine in a personal, relational way.

103

Reflective questions arise naturally from this journey. How does the heart recognize truth in thought, word, and action? Where do experiences of goodness guide decisions and shape character? How is love recognized and extended in ways that resonate with the eternal call for relational connection? Each reflection opens the soul to a deeper understanding, preparing it to perceive Christ not only as an abstract ideal but as the living fulfillment of what Satyam and Shivam have long promised.

The human journey, then, is a movement from fragments and shadows toward fullness. Satyam and Shivam appear as glimpses, guiding the heart along paths of insight and ethical living. Christam represents the fulfillment, bringing relational presence, moral clarity, and transformative love. This triad is a roadmap for the soul, integrating aspiration, ethical engagement, and relational depth into the life-long pursuit of the Eternal.

10.1 Satyam — Glimpses of Eternal Truth

Human beings encounter truth not only through study or observation but in the quiet stirrings of conscience and reflection. There are moments when the heart recognizes what is genuinely real and trustworthy, a sense of alignment with something enduring that transcends personal desire. In the Vedic tradition, **Ṛta** represents this cosmic order, an underlying truth that sustains the universe and establishes the proper alignment of action, speech, and thought. Observing life and its moral patterns can reveal glimpses of this order, showing that truth is not arbitrary but woven into the fabric of existence.

The Upanishads provide a philosophical lens for understanding eternal truth. Brahman is described as the ultimate reality, unchanging, infinite, and the source of all consciousness. Reflection on Brahman encourages the seeker to recognize that beneath the shifting appearances of life lies a stable, eternal principle. Human moral insight resonates with this notion: the recognition of right and wrong, the intuitive awareness of justice, honesty, and integrity are echoes of the eternal truth in our hearts. These moments of discernment awaken the conscience, guiding decisions and shaping character.

Experiences of Satyam often appear subtly in daily life. A sudden recognition that a course of action aligns with honesty, a deep intuition that one should act with fairness, or the feeling of peace when speaking truthfully are all encounters with fragments of eternal truth. These experiences cultivate awareness that truth is relational, guiding how one interacts with others and how one understands reality. Ethical reflection and intellectual inquiry together prepare the mind to perceive the fullness of truth in the Word, who embodies the eternal principle.

The Word as Logos reveals Satyam in its entirety. The truth glimpsed in conscience, moral reflection, and philosophical insight is now personified in the Word, inviting a relational encounter with the eternal reality. The preparation of the mind and heart through attention to truth, ethical discernment, and contemplation aligns the seeker to recognize the Word not merely as a teacher of truths but as the living embodiment of truth itself.

Human experience demonstrates that these glimpses of Satyam are formative. They awaken the heart to recognize the value of integrity, to seek what is right over what is convenient, and to cultivate attentiveness to both ethical and spiritual realities. Through reflection, moral intuition, and openness to insight, the human soul is drawn toward the fulfillment of these experiences, anticipating the relational and incarnate presence of the Word as the ultimate realization of truth.

10.2 Shivam — Moral Goodness and Virtue

Moral goodness is visible when human actions align with ethical principles that transcend personal gain. In Hindu texts, dharma embodies this alignment, directing individuals toward responsibilities, fairness, and care for others. Living according to dharma cultivates inner harmony and contributes to social cohesion, showing that virtue is both personal and relational. Compassion and ahimsa extend this ethical framework, guiding behavior toward non-violence, empathy, and attentiveness to the well-being of all living beings. Ethical living is thus a mirror of the eternal goodness that undergirds the universe.

Daily life offers countless opportunities to encounter this moral goodness. Acts of care for family, fairness in professional responsibilities, patience with friends, or forgiveness toward those who have wronged us provide concrete experiences of virtue. These moments shape character, fostering sensitivity, empathy, and self-discipline. Ethical decisions, even when difficult, train the heart to perceive what is just and loving, forming a foundation for relational awareness and spiritual receptivity.

Virtue is not merely outward compliance but an internal cultivation of character. The texts highlight that the inner orientation of the mind and heart determines the authenticity of ethical action.

For instance, the Bhagavad Gita emphasizes acting according to dharma without attachment to personal reward, showing that moral excellence is relational, grounded in awareness of a higher principle that guides human conduct. This ethical cultivation shapes the heart for the fullness of relational life that comes with encountering the eternal Word.

Human striving toward virtue anticipates the embodiment of perfect goodness. By living with compassion, integrity, and justice, individuals experience reflections of the eternal moral order. These practices open the heart, training it to recognize the ultimate source of goodness when it manifests personally in the Word. Virtuous living is therefore not an end in itself but a preparation for deeper relational encounter, forming the soul to respond to divine guidance with discernment, love, and commitment.

Through ethical reflection, attentiveness to conscience, and dedication to moral growth, humans cultivate a living awareness of Shivam. The presence of virtue in daily actions becomes a guide, showing the heart how to align with goodness, how to exercise care, and how to engage relationally with the eternal reality. Each act of ethical courage, forgiveness, or compassionate service illuminates the pathway toward relational fulfillment, making moral striving a tangible preparation for experiencing the fullness of divine goodness in the incarnate Word.

10.3 Christam — Jesus Christ as Fullness

Christ represents the culmination of truth and goodness, bringing to completion what the human heart has been glimpsing in conscience, ethical striving, and relational longing. In the Gospel of John, Christ is described as the Logos, the eternal Word through whom life, light, and moral clarity enter human history. This Word is not abstract but personal and active, engaging hearts, guiding moral understanding, and inviting relationship. Through Christ, the ideals of truth and virtue become embodied in a living presence accessible to human experience.

The life of Christ demonstrates the fullness of goodness in action. Through teaching, healing, and acts of mercy, Christ shows what it means to live in alignment with eternal truth while embodying moral excellence. Stories such as the calling of the first disciples reveal relational openness and trust as central to following this path. Christ's words and deeds guide ethical discernment, providing concrete examples of how the heart can respond faithfully to the eternal moral order while engaging in compassionate service.

Relational love is central to Christ's presence. In interactions with followers, neighbors, and those marginalized, Christ embodies a love that is patient, sacrificial, and transformative. By modeling forgiveness, care, and relational attentiveness, Christ demonstrates that ultimate goodness is inseparable from love and relational commitment. Human experience is invited into this dynamic, learning to mirror such love in daily life, cultivating trust, empathy, and responsiveness to moral insight.

Recognition of Christ as the fulfillment of truth and virtue awakens the heart to a deeper relational awareness. The call to trust and relational openness invites individuals to respond freely, integrating conscience, moral striving, and devotional longing. Encounters with Christ provide clarity where partial glimpses once left longing, revealing how the eternal principles of Satyam and Shivam find tangible fulfillment in a personal, relational presence.

Through the Gospels, the actions of Christ—teaching, healing, forgiving, and guiding—illustrate a life where truth, goodness, and love converge. Human response becomes a matter of relational participation: recognizing Christ as the Word made flesh, responding in faith, and cultivating openness to ongoing transformation. In this way, Christ embodies the fullness of what conscience, virtue, and longing have prepared the heart to receive, uniting moral insight, ethical formation, and relational love into a living, accessible reality.

10.4 Integrating the Triad in Daily Life

Daily life becomes a canvas where the principles of Satyam, Shivam, and Christam intersect in meaningful and practical ways. Pursuit of truth, or Satyam, manifests in decisions guided by conscience, ethical reflection, and careful discernment. Every choice, from honesty in communication to integrity in work, is an opportunity to recognize what is right and real. These moments, though ordinary, reveal a responsiveness to the eternal truth that forms the foundation of moral life.

Living in goodness, or Shivam, complements the pursuit of truth by shaping actions with compassion, justice, and care for others. Ethical ideals are not abstract principles but are expressed in the ways individuals interact with family, neighbors, and broader communities. Acts of kindness, patience in challenging situations, and forgiveness toward those who have wronged us exemplify how virtue becomes a lived experience. Ethical discernment, motivated by concern for others, becomes both a personal discipline and a relational encounter with goodness.

Encountering Christ, or Christam, brings relational fullness to the pursuit of truth and moral excellence. Daily moments of prayer, reflection, reading, and communal life allow Christ's presence to illuminate ethical choices and relational interactions. Christ as the Logos engages the heart, guiding understanding and inspiring actions that reflect relational love and moral clarity. Experiences of mercy, encouragement, and relational attentiveness mirror Christ's teaching, making the eternal triad tangible in ordinary contexts.

The integration of truth, goodness, and relational encounter transforms the ordinary into opportunities for spiritual and ethical growth. A moment of moral courage at work, a compassionate response to a friend in need, or a reflective prayer in solitude can all become expressions of the triad. Personal experience functions as a microcosm of this larger reality: conscience, virtue, and relational openness converge, inviting the heart to participate actively in the life and moral order revealed through Christ. By attending to these ordinary instances, individuals cultivate a life that embodies the principles of Satyam, Shivam, and Christam in both action and awareness.

In relationships, the triad guides communication, forgiveness, and empathetic listening, reinforcing how moral truth and goodness are inseparable from relational presence. Decisions grounded in reflection and ethical insight strengthen trust and deepen bonds, allowing the heart to experience the fullness of what it has long sought. Ordinary life thus becomes a laboratory for spiritual and moral formation, where the triad is not theoretical but experienced dynamically through attentive, loving, and truth-oriented engagement.

Through consistent practice, attention, and openness, the integration of Satyam, Shivam, and Christam shapes both character and relational awareness. Each encounter with ethical choice, moral challenge, or relational opportunity becomes a touchpoint where eternal principles are experienced concretely. In this way, the triad serves not only as a framework for reflection but as a living guide that transforms daily life, fostering alignment of heart, conscience, and action with the fullness of truth, goodness, and relational love.

10.5 Contemplation and Relational Awareness

Contemplation offers a vital space for the heart and mind to engage deeply with the triad of Satyam, Shivam, and Christam. In quiet reflection, individuals can notice the ways truth, goodness, and relational love intersect in their lives. Moments of prayer, meditation, or journaling allow the heart to pause and attend to these convergences, revealing patterns of ethical insight and relational responsiveness that might otherwise go unnoticed. Awareness of these convergences nurtures a sensitivity to the presence of Christ in ordinary circumstances, illuminating how ethical choices and moral discernment are embedded in everyday life.

Human experience offers many avenues for cultivating this awareness. Reflection on personal decisions, ethical challenges, and relational interactions encourages recognition of where truth has guided action and where goodness has shaped response. Journaling allows individuals to track moments of insight, mercy, or courage, creating a record of how Christ's relational love influences both perception and behavior. Contemplation also fosters an attunement to conscience, helping individuals identify ways in which relational love can guide choices, deepen empathy, and strengthen commitment to moral principles.

Prayer acts as a relational dialogue that integrates reflection and ethical awareness. By addressing Christ directly, individuals situate their daily life within the framework of relational love, aligning intentions with moral and spiritual truths. Acts of gratitude, intercession, or silent listening enhance the perception of Christ's presence, encouraging a responsiveness that extends from the inner life to outward action. Ethical reflection during these practices reinforces the dynamic connection between awareness of goodness and concrete expressions of virtue, linking inner formation to lived reality.

In daily life, relational knowledge of Christ manifests in the alignment of thought, word, and deed. Awareness of truth guides understanding, attentiveness to goodness informs interactions, and openness to relational love fosters compassionate engagement with others. Contemplative practice strengthens the capacity to perceive these dimensions simultaneously, revealing the triad not as abstract ideals but as realities that shape choices, relationships, and moral vision.

Repeated attention to moments of reflection and meditation cultivates an integrated perspective where ethical discernment, relational responsiveness, and spiritual awareness reinforce each other. Individuals learn to recognize signs of Christ's presence in ordinary experiences, from acts of service to moments of quiet insight. This practice transforms both inner life and outward action, allowing the triad to guide decisions, relationships, and personal growth consistently. By fostering awareness through contemplation, the heart matures in its capacity to perceive and participate in the fullness of truth, goodness, and relational love.

Conclusion: Satyam, Shivam, Christam as Life Orientation

The triad of Satyam, Shivam, and Christam offers a holistic orientation for living that engages the mind, heart, and conscience. Satyam, or eternal truth, provides a foundation for discerning reality, understanding moral principles, and cultivating intellectual clarity. It invites reflection on what is right, enduring, and aligned with the order of creation. Human experience reveals that moments of insight, ethical reasoning, and intuitive recognition of truth serve as guides in decision-making and moral judgment, preparing the heart to encounter deeper fulfillment.

Shivam emphasizes moral goodness and virtue in action. Living in accordance with dharma, compassion, and ethical principles shapes character and cultivates relational sensitivity. Acts of care, forgiveness, justice, and self-discipline reflect this goodness and create opportunities for the heart to engage with the moral dimension of life. Ethical striving opens pathways for relational encounters, nurturing the capacity to respond to others with empathy, integrity, and attentiveness. Human experience demonstrates that virtues are not merely abstract ideals but lived realities that guide conduct and illuminate the moral order.

Christam represents the culmination of this journey, embodying truth and goodness in relational, personal presence. Encountering Christ integrates intellectual clarity and ethical formation with relational love and trust. The Gospels illustrate how teaching, healing, and compassionate engagement manifest both truth and goodness in tangible, relational ways. Human response to Christ involves recognition, trust, and openness, enabling the heart to participate in the fullness of life that these longings anticipate.

Reflective questions can guide daily awareness and application. Where is eternal truth shaping your choices, guiding your understanding, and informing your ethical discernment? How does goodness influence your relationships, interactions, and moral decisions? In what ways does Christ embody the fulfillment of the deepest longings of your heart, providing relational, ethical, and spiritual orientation?

By integrating Satyam, Shivam, and Christam as a framework, the human heart is invited into an ongoing journey of discovery, moral alignment, and relational participation. This triad orients life toward enduring realities, enabling a living engagement with truth, goodness, and love, and fostering a rhythm of reflection, ethical action, and relational openness that transforms both inner life and outward conduct.

Chapter 11: Walking in Truth and Love

Human life is naturally oriented toward fulfillment, yet true fulfillment is not found solely in material success, social recognition, or fleeting pleasures. There is a deeper dimension within the human heart that longs for alignment with truth, ethical integrity, and relational love. This longing surfaces in conscience, in the desire to act rightly, and in the pursuit of meaningful relationships that honor both oneself and others. These inclinations point toward a life that transcends mere survival or comfort, inviting the heart to participate in a reality that is enduring, trustworthy, and relationally rich.

Christ embodies the fullness of truth and love, making these ideals tangible and personally accessible. Through his teachings, life, and actions, truth is not abstract or distant but lived and relational. His moral guidance provides clarity for navigating the complexities of human existence, offering a standard that is consistent, wise, and compassionate. Similarly, love is not presented merely as a principle but as a way of being that engages the heart, fosters empathy, and transforms relationships. In this way, Christ unites ethical living and relational depth, showing that a life rooted in truth and love is both coherent and vibrant.

Everyday life provides countless opportunities to engage with truth and love. Decisions at work, care for family members, interactions with friends, and acts of service in the community are all arenas where the heart exercises discernment and expresses relational commitment. The capacity to respond faithfully in these moments reflects an awareness of the moral and relational order that Christ reveals. Ethical choices become opportunities to practice integrity, while relational engagement becomes a medium for expressing love that mirrors the divine character.

Reflective questions invite careful attention to one's own life. How does your daily routine reflect adherence to truth, both in thought and action? In what ways do acts of love guide your relationships, shape your decisions, and influence your community? Are moments of ethical clarity and compassionate engagement present in your ordinary interactions? These questions encourage the reader to notice that living in truth and love is not an abstract ideal but an ongoing practice that emerges in concrete, relational contexts.

The human heart's longing for meaning and ethical coherence finds both direction and fulfillment in walking a path shaped by relational truth and active love. Ethical ideals and moral insights are not ends in themselves but invitations to participate in a life that is both morally upright and intimately relational. Christ illuminates this path, showing that truth guides understanding and choice, while love deepens engagement with others and nurtures a heart attuned to the Eternal. Living oriented toward truth and love therefore involves attentive awareness, ethical discernment, and a responsive heart that seeks to reflect divine goodness in all facets of daily life.

Verifiable references include the Gospel of John, where Christ presents himself as the way, the truth, and the source of abundant life (John 14:6; John 10:10), and the ethical teachings found in his parables, such as the Good Samaritan (Luke 10:25–37), which illustrate relational love in practical contexts. These scriptural passages demonstrate that truth and love are not distant ideals but active realities meant to shape human life and interaction.

11.1 Ethical Living in the Light of Christ

Ethical living reaches its fullest expression when moral ideals are grounded in the relational presence of Christ. Principles such as dharma, satya, and ahimsa, which guide duty, truthfulness, and non-harm, become personally meaningful and transformative when oriented toward the relational reality of Christ's life and teaching. In daily life, these ethical standards are not abstract rules but invitations to align thought, word, and action with a moral order that is both just and compassionate. The heart becomes attuned to recognizing what is right, what fosters human flourishing, and what expresses care for others in practical ways.

In the workplace, ethical living manifests in honesty, fairness, and respect for colleagues. Decisions are informed by integrity rather than convenience, and interactions honor the dignity of all involved. For example, a manager who chooses transparency over self-interest models dharma in a way that resonates with the ethical depth revealed in both Hindu moral reflection and Christ's teaching on honesty and righteousness.

Family life provides another arena where ethical ideals find expression. Patience, forgiveness, and attentive care reflect ahimsa in relational contexts. Upholding commitments, nurturing children with guidance and love, and resolving conflicts through understanding rather than dominance all embody ethical responsiveness that flows from Christ's relational model. Everyday choices in the home mirror the ethical shadows discussed in earlier chapters, now perfected and fulfilled in Christ's relational presence. Community engagement highlights justice and care as central components of ethical living. Acts of service, advocacy for the marginalized, and participation in charitable initiatives translate moral principles into concrete action. By responding to the needs of neighbors, society, and the vulnerable, individuals cultivate virtues that echo dharma and satya while participating in the active love revealed in Christ. Ethical living becomes a tangible expression of relational trust, concern, and accountability.

Human examples illustrate how ethical responsiveness is both attainable and transformative. A teacher who goes beyond instruction to mentor students models integrity and relational responsibility. A healthcare worker providing care with compassion demonstrates the union of moral ideals and love in action. Communities that embrace ethical conduct as a shared value reflect how moral awareness and relational engagement shape human life in a profound, ongoing way.

Scriptural grounding reinforces these principles. Christ's teachings on the Greatest Commandment to love God and neighbor (Matthew 22:37–40) encapsulate the integration of ethical observance and relational devotion. The parable of the Good Samaritan (Luke 10:25–37) exemplifies moral responsiveness that transcends social convention, showing that ethical action rooted in relational love brings tangible flourishing. By living ethically in light of Christ, moral ideals are no longer distant aspirations but active realities that shape daily experience, nurture conscience, and foster relational depth.

11.2 Love as Action and Presence

Love reaches its fullest expression when it is lived as action rather than remaining a mere sentiment. Relational love calls for engagement, presence, and responsiveness to the needs of others. Christ demonstrates love not as a passive feeling but as tangible service, attentive care, and reconciliation with those who are marginalized, suffering, or estranged. His interactions in the Gospels reveal that love is inseparable from action, guiding moral and relational decisions with wisdom and compassion. In John 13:1–17, the washing of the disciples' feet illustrates love as humility and service, showing that authentic care often requires self-giving and intentional effort.

In human life, this model translates into everyday choices. Acts of empathy, listening attentively, offering support to those in distress, and responding to injustice are all concrete expressions of relational love. For example, helping a neighbor in difficulty, mentoring someone in need of guidance, or mediating conflict within a community demonstrates how love shapes ethical behavior. Such actions cultivate moral courage, requiring individuals to step beyond comfort zones and respond to the needs of others with integrity and compassion.

Reconciliation forms another dimension of love in action. Forgiving those who have caused harm, seeking to restore broken relationships, and practicing patience in tension-filled situations reflect Christ's teaching on mercy and relational restoration. In Luke 15, the parable of the prodigal son illustrates the transformative power of love to heal, welcome, and restore. Human experience mirrors this principle when individuals extend forgiveness and embrace restorative practices within families, workplaces, and communities.

Service becomes a tangible avenue for demonstrating love. Volunteering time and resources, advocating for justice, and standing with the oppressed embody the ethical and relational dimensions of love emphasized in prior chapters. These actions not only assist others but also shape the character of the one who gives, nurturing empathy, humility, and relational sensitivity. Love becomes a lived practice that aligns moral awareness with action.

Christ's relational presence teaches that love is inseparable from attentiveness and moral discernment. Loving others involves recognizing their needs, discerning what actions promote flourishing, and committing to sustained engagement. Ethical courage arises when individuals act with integrity even when faced with opposition or sacrifice. Through service, empathy, and reconciliation, love transforms ordinary life into a space where divine goodness and relational care are expressed and received.

In daily experience, these principles cultivate communities that reflect both moral order and relational harmony. Families, workplaces, and neighborhoods become arenas for the active practice of love, where ethical behavior and compassionate engagement reinforce each other. By living love as action and presence, the ideals of truth and goodness become inseparable from the relational reality of care, bringing moral and spiritual life into concrete expression.

11.3 Conscience and Moral Discernment

Conscience serves as an inner guide that shapes human decisions and aligns actions with truth and goodness. It operates as a subtle, intuitive awareness of what is right and wrong, providing moral clarity even before formal reasoning or external instruction. The relational framework of truth, as experienced through Christ, enhances the conscience by showing that ethical discernment is not merely a personal preference but a response to the moral order inherent in creation and revealed in relational engagement with God.

Reflection and prayer are central to cultivating moral insight. Taking time to pause and consider decisions, examining intentions, and seeking divine guidance help the heart recognize what is just, compassionate, and true. In Philippians 4:8, attention to whatever is true, noble, and right directs the mind and heart toward ethical action, reinforcing that conscience is shaped by ongoing attentiveness to relational truth. Journaling, meditation, or silent contemplation often bring patterns into awareness, highlighting recurring moral intuitions that can guide daily choices.

Human experience demonstrates the practical role of conscience in everyday situations. A person deciding whether to speak up against injustice at work, choosing how to respond to a neighbor in need, or navigating conflict in family life may feel an inner prompt that guides toward ethical action. Listening to this moral awareness requires courage and humility, as the prompt may challenge comfort or personal advantage. In such moments, reflection on past experiences, ethical principles, and attentiveness to the needs of others strengthens discernment and moral clarity.

Conscience also interacts with relational love. Ethical choices are most authentic when they serve both truth and the well-being of others. In moments of decision, the heart must weigh the consequences for relationships, justice, and mercy. Acts of forgiveness, standing with the vulnerable, or responding compassionately to moral failures in others illustrate how conscience integrates moral awareness with practical love. Each act reflects alignment with the deeper order that truth and goodness embody in relational life.

Scenarios of ethical discernment reveal how conscience directs action without coercion. A teacher navigating fairness in grading, a leader deciding on equitable distribution of resources, or a friend offering counsel may experience inner promptings that encourage justice, patience, and integrity. These nudges are not abstract but relational, emphasizing that ethical awareness responds to human needs and divine guidance simultaneously.

Over time, attentive cultivation of conscience strengthens the capacity for discernment and moral courage. Ethical sensitivity deepens, enabling individuals to recognize subtle injustices, act with empathy, and navigate complex relational dynamics with integrity. The conscience becomes a lived faculty, continually refining moral perception and informing loving action in the world.

11.4 Integrating Truth and Love in Daily Practices

Daily life provides countless opportunities to live in alignment with truth and love. Ethical awareness is not confined to extraordinary decisions or grand gestures but can be expressed through ordinary routines and responsibilities. Each task, conversation, or interaction carries the potential to reflect both moral clarity and relational care when approached with attention and intentionality.

Mindful conversation is one way truth and love converge. Listening attentively, responding honestly, and showing respect in dialogue cultivate trust and understanding. In Ephesians 4:25, the call to speak truthfully is connected with fostering community and relational integrity. By aligning words with truth and considering the impact on others, communication becomes an act of ethical and relational engagement.

Honest work extends ethical practice into professional life. Performing duties with diligence, transparency, and accountability demonstrates integrity and respect for the well-being of others. Acts of honesty in the workplace, such as fair dealings, acknowledging contributions, or taking responsibility for mistakes, exemplify how ordinary responsibilities become occasions for moral reflection and relational awareness. Colossians 3:23 encourages working wholeheartedly as for the Lord, which frames even routine labor as an expression of virtue and love.

Compassionate service highlights relational love in action. Helping neighbors, supporting colleagues, or volunteering for the vulnerable reflects sensitivity to human needs and embodies ethical principles in tangible ways. Ethical ideals are made concrete through acts of service, illustrating how love and justice complement each other in lived experience. Every small gesture of assistance or encouragement strengthens relationships and affirms the moral order present in human life.

Relational care within family, community, and social networks integrates truth and love in a sustained manner. Respecting boundaries, listening to emotions, fostering fairness, and practicing forgiveness exemplify living truthfully and lovingly. These interactions create environments where moral discernment and relational attentiveness mutually reinforce each other, guiding daily choices toward both ethical and compassionate action.

In daily practices, there is a seamless connection between moral clarity and relational responsiveness. Ethical awareness informs how one engages with others, while relational sensitivity ensures that actions align with deeper truths. Whether in conversation, work, service, or care, ordinary life becomes a canvas for expressing the integration of truth and love. Through these practices, the heart gradually internalizes ethical and relational principles, demonstrating that moral discernment and relational engagement are inseparable components of human flourishing.

11.5 Transformation of Character and Heart

Walking in truth and love has a profound impact on personal character and spiritual awareness. Ethical principles, when actively embodied, shape the inner life, cultivating qualities that refine the heart and guide relational engagement. The process of living morally and lovingly is transformative because it aligns actions, intentions, and desires with the moral and relational order that reflects the Eternal.

Patience emerges as one learns to respond to others with understanding rather than immediate judgment. Situations that test tolerance, such as disagreements or unexpected setbacks, provide opportunities to practice restraint and thoughtful consideration. Galatians 5:22 highlights patience as a fruit of the Spirit, demonstrating that growth in virtue flows from persistent engagement with ethical and relational practices.

Forgiveness illustrates the integration of truth and love in personal transformation. Choosing to release resentment and extend grace strengthens relationships and restores moral harmony. Human experience shows that forgiveness is both a challenge and a pathway to freedom, reshaping the heart to reflect deeper compassion and relational awareness. Ephesians 4:32 connects forgiveness with kindness and empathy, revealing the relational dimension of ethical growth.

Empathy deepens as one recognizes the struggles and emotions of others. Attentive listening, understanding perspectives, and responding to needs develop moral sensitivity and relational attunement. Experiencing the vulnerability of others fosters moral imagination, allowing ethical principles to move from abstract ideas to lived realities.

Courage and humility are interwoven in the transformation of character. Courage allows one to uphold truth and act with integrity even when faced with pressure or opposition. Humility ensures that ethical action is grounded in service rather than self-interest. Together, these qualities support relational maturation by promoting justice, care, and mutual respect.

Through continuous engagement in truth and love, the heart evolves. Ethical growth nurtures relational sensitivity, and relational experiences refine moral discernment. Human character and spiritual awareness develop not in isolation but in interaction with the world and with others, reflecting the integrated nature of moral, intellectual, and relational formation. The journey of transformation demonstrates that walking in truth and love shapes the self into a living expression of both ethical clarity and relational depth, preparing the heart to embody the fullness of the Eternal in daily life.

11.6 Community and Relational Impact

Living in truth and love extends beyond personal transformation to shape families, friendships, and broader communities. Ethical and loving actions create a ripple effect, influencing others not by force but by the example of integrity and care. When individuals embody these principles, relationships gain depth, trust strengthens, and a culture of mutual respect develops.

In family life, truth and love foster honesty, patience, and attentive care. Parents and children who practice ethical awareness and relational empathy create an environment where guidance and correction are offered with understanding. Siblings and spouses who engage in transparent communication and compassionate action model the relational dimensions of moral living. Human experience consistently shows that families grounded in ethical and loving principles cultivate resilience, emotional well-being, and mutual support.

Friendships flourish when truth and love guide interactions. Listening with attentiveness, offering help without expectation, and practicing forgiveness strengthen bonds and create safe spaces for personal growth. Acts of loyalty, honesty, and generosity reinforce relational trust, encouraging friends to pursue ethical choices in their own lives. The Gospels illustrate relational impact through the disciples' formation, showing how individual alignment with truth and love inspires collective growth.

In the broader society, ethical and loving behavior fosters justice, fairness, and social harmony. Mentoring and ethical leadership provide guidance for younger generations and peers, demonstrating that principles of care and integrity are practical and achievable. Reconciliation efforts in communities, whether through dialogue, service, or mediation, reflect the outward expression of personal moral formation. Human history shows that communities where members actively live out truth and love experience reduced conflict, increased cooperation, and flourishing relationships.

Each act of ethical and loving engagement, no matter how small, contributes to a network of influence. Choices rooted in moral discernment and relational awareness inspire others to act similarly, creating a culture where justice, mercy, and compassion thrive. By participating in this communal dimension, individuals discover that living in truth and love is both a personal journey and a relational vocation, connecting hearts, strengthening bonds, and extending the presence of the Eternal into daily life.

11.7 Spiritual Awareness in Daily Life

Awareness of Christ's presence in everyday life transforms ordinary moments into opportunities for reflection, moral insight, and relational connection. Spiritual attentiveness does not require extraordinary circumstances; rather, it emerges in simple acts of mindfulness, thoughtful conversation, and ethical decision-making. Recognizing the relational guidance available in daily experiences allows the heart to align more fully with truth and love.

Prayer and reflection serve as practices that deepen this awareness. Regular moments of dialogue with God, whether in formal prayer or silent meditation, cultivate attentiveness to the moral and relational dynamics present in each situation. Scripture reading and contemplation of Christ's life provide tangible examples of how ethical principles and relational love are enacted, offering models for integrating these values into ordinary routines.

Attentive living encourages noticing subtle indications of divine presence. A gesture of kindness, a decision made with integrity, or an opportunity for forgiveness can be understood as reflections of Christ's guidance. By intentionally observing these moments, individuals strengthen their capacity to respond with ethical discernment and relational love. This practice fosters a rhythm where daily life itself becomes a canvas for spiritual growth, demonstrating that ordinary actions and awareness are pathways through which truth and love are continuously encountered.

Human experience confirms that integrating prayer, reflection, and attentiveness nurtures resilience, empathy, and moral clarity. Each encounter, each choice, and each observation can be understood as a dialogue with the Eternal, revealing that spiritual awareness in daily life is both accessible and transformative, shaping character and guiding relationships toward wholeness.

11.8 Sustaining the Path

Walking consistently in truth and love presents real challenges. Life often brings moments of moral uncertainty, interpersonal conflict, or personal weakness that can make sustaining ethical and relational commitments difficult. These setbacks, however, are not indications of failure but opportunities for growth, reflection, and renewed dedication to living faithfully.

Persistence requires humility, acknowledging that the path toward ethical and relational maturity is ongoing. Reflection allows the heart to examine choices, understand missteps, and gain insight into areas needing adjustment. Forgiveness, both of self and others, restores relational balance and clears the way for continued engagement in love. Accountability within relationships provides support and guidance, offering encouragement and perspective when individual efforts falter.

Human experience provides many examples of resilience and ethical consistency. Individuals who navigate workplace challenges with integrity, families who restore trust after conflict, and communities that rebuild cooperation after division all illustrate the sustaining power of relational commitment guided by truth and love. These lived experiences demonstrate that ethical and spiritual formation is not linear but requires continual attentiveness, patience, and the willingness to learn from difficulties. The practice of sustaining the path strengthens moral character and deepens relational awareness, enabling the heart to remain aligned with divine guidance over time.

Conclusion: Life as Walking in Light and Love

Living in the light of truth and love means allowing the presence and guidance of Christ to shape every aspect of daily life. When moral ideals are pursued not as abstract rules but as lived expressions of relational awareness, the heart experiences both fulfillment and alignment with what is good and true. Acts of love, whether in small gestures of care, honesty in relationships, or courageous ethical decisions, reflect the active presence of divine guidance and transform ordinary interactions into moments of spiritual significance.

Reflective questions help the heart notice this transformation. How is truth influencing your choices today? In what ways do acts of love shape your relationships and interactions? Which daily practices, whether in work, family life, or personal reflection, open your awareness to the ongoing presence of God? Attentiveness to these questions fosters a deeper sensitivity to moral and relational realities and encourages intentional participation in life guided by love and truth.

Walking in this way is not a finite task but a lifelong engagement. Each moment presents opportunities to practice patience, empathy, forgiveness, and moral courage, gradually forming character and deepening relational awareness. Life lived as walking in light and love becomes a dynamic path of transformation, where ethical ideals and relational yearning converge, and the heart continually grows in harmony with the eternal reality revealed in Christ.

Chapter 12: Rivers Meet — Harmony and Fulfillment

The human heart has always been like a river, flowing with longing that is at once personal and universal. This longing takes many forms: the desire for truth that clarifies our choices, the yearning for goodness that shapes our actions, and the quest for love that completes and sustains us relationally. These currents of longing often begin as small streams, emerging in conscience, ethical intuition, or spiritual insight. They appear in moments when we feel awe in creation, when we recognize the injustice in the world and are moved to act, or when we sense a presence beyond ourselves calling us toward something greater. These streams, though originating in separate experiences and disciplines, share a common destination: the human heart seeks fullness, harmony, and relational encounter with the Eternal.

Across cultures and centuries, glimpses of this fullness have appeared in moral ideals, devotional practices, and philosophical reflection. In the Vedic and Upanishadic traditions, the heart perceives cosmic order, dharma, and the call of Brahman as a guiding light. In Bhakti poetry, the soul experiences yearning for a personal, loving divine presence. In each instance, the human spirit catches a shadow of what it was made to know, pointing toward a deeper reality that transcends abstract teaching or ritual. These shadows, while partial, illuminate the pathways of conscience and devotion, preparing the heart to recognize the One who embodies the truth, goodness, and love that have been sought across time and space.

The convergence of these currents is not merely symbolic. When ethical striving, spiritual insight, and relational yearning meet the fullness of Christ, they flow into a single, transforming ocean of life. Christ does not merely represent an idea or ideal; Christ is the personal reality in which the heart's longings find their ultimate satisfaction. Recognition of this relational encounter begins with attentiveness: noticing where truth clarifies decisions, where goodness shapes conduct, and where love calls for relational engagement. The human heart is invited to respond naturally, not coerced, as each prior glimpse and shadow comes together into a coherent vision of the Eternal.

Reflective questions arise for the reader: How do the currents of your life experiences point toward ultimate fulfillment? In what ways do moments of ethical awareness, moral courage, and relational longing reveal a deeper invitation? Can you see the convergence of truth, goodness, and love in your own heart, quietly guiding your choices and relationships? These reflections are not abstract exercises but invitations to recognize that the journey of the human spirit, with all its seeking and striving, is meeting its intended fulfillment in relational union with the Eternal.

The imagery of rivers flowing toward a vast ocean reminds us that no matter how winding or fragmented the paths of life may appear, all currents of longing, insight, and desire have a destination. The streams of conscience, devotion, and ethical striving are not isolated—they converge in Christ, who embodies the fullness of what the heart has been pursuing. This convergence sets the stage for the following sections, where the transformation of longing into relational reality, the harmonizing of human experience, and the integration of moral, spiritual, and relational life will be explored in greater depth.

Human experience confirms this dynamic. In moments of awe, grief, compassion, and moral reflection, we sense the presence of a guiding hand, a relational reality that calls us beyond ourselves. These encounters are invitations to step into the ocean of fulfillment where truth illuminates, goodness shapes, and love embraces. Every act of ethical discernment, every choice to respond with compassion, and every effort to pursue relational depth becomes part of the flowing river, merging into the eternal current that offers completion and wholeness to the human heart.

This opening chapter of convergence reminds the reader that the human journey is inherently relational. The currents of seeking are not wandering aimlessly; they are oriented by God's design toward relational encounter and fullness. The heart, attentive and willing, can perceive where truth clarifies, goodness guides, and love completes. Here, the rivers meet, and the human spirit begins to drink from the ocean of life that satisfies every longing, illuminates every uncertainty, and perfects every ethical pursuit.

12.1 The River of Longing

Human longing is a current that flows silently yet persistently through every life, shaping thoughts, choices, and aspirations. From childhood, the heart senses incompleteness and seeks meaning beyond the immediate and material. People long for security, for protection from harm, and for a life that carries significance beyond mere survival. This desire often expresses itself in the pursuit of moral ideals, ethical living, and relational depth, showing that the human spirit is oriented toward something enduring and trustworthy. Forgiveness and reconciliation emerge as natural responses to relational brokenness, highlighting the innate yearning to restore harmony and connection with others.

Across cultures and history, these longings have found articulation in stories, songs, and sacred texts. Ancient civilizations recorded moral codes, philosophical reflections, and devotional practices as ways to channel the heart's desire toward a greater reality. In the Upanishads, the human spirit is called to recognize Brahman as the ultimate ground of being, inviting reflection on truth and unity. The Bhagavad Gita presents a vision of dharma and righteous action as a response to the soul's awareness of higher purpose. Bhakti poetry captures the intimate ache for divine closeness, portraying the human desire for love, protection, and relational intimacy as both passionate and personal.

Everyday life provides vivid illustrations of this river of longing. A parent prays silently for the wellbeing of a child, a friend reaches out to reconcile after a disagreement, and an individual sits in contemplation, sensing an inner call to live rightly. Moments of ethical decision-making, moral reflection, and attentive love reveal that these currents are not abstract or distant; they are alive in human conscience and relational awareness. Even in times of uncertainty or suffering, the heart recognizes a presence beyond itself that invites trust and hope.

The river of longing thus carries multiple streams: the pursuit of moral clarity, the search for relational restoration, and the yearning for spiritual fulfillment. Each stream shows the natural orientation of the human heart toward a source of goodness and truth that transcends the self. These longings are more than emotional impulses; they are indicators of the human spirit's capacity to encounter the Eternal. By observing and attending to these currents, one begins to see a pattern: the deepest desires of the heart point toward fulfillment that is personal, relational, and transformative, inviting the human spirit into a flow that exceeds the ordinary.

12.2 The River of Insight

The river of insight flows alongside the river of longing, carrying with it tributaries of understanding, reflection, and moral awareness. Human beings are naturally equipped with conscience, the inner sense of right and wrong, which guides decisions and illuminates ethical pathways. Intuition often signals what is true and just before reasoning can fully grasp it. Across cultures, this moral sensitivity has been nurtured through ethical codes, philosophical inquiry, and devotional practices. The Vedic concept of dharma, for instance, provides guidance for righteous living, offering a framework through which individuals can align action with the good. Similarly, the Upanishadic emphasis on self-knowledge and reflection encourages discernment of ultimate reality and the cultivation of inner clarity.

Human experience demonstrates how insight functions as a living stream. Moments of ethical courage, such as standing for justice or acting with integrity despite risk, reveal the subtle ways the heart is attuned to higher principles. Reflective clarity emerges in meditation, study, or contemplative prayer, allowing the mind and conscience to perceive patterns of truth and goodness that might otherwise remain hidden. Devotional acts, such as surrender, compassion, and service, further cultivate relational awareness, connecting ethical insight with the lived reality of love. These tributaries converge to prepare the heart for recognition of ultimate truth, forming a landscape where moral understanding and relational sensitivity coalesce.

Even ordinary situations can reveal the river's flow. A decision to forgive, to help someone in need, or to act honestly in challenging circumstances manifests the undercurrent of ethical and spiritual insight. These experiences show that the pursuit of truth is not merely theoretical; it is woven into the fabric of daily life. As individuals attend to these currents of conscience, intuition, and virtue, the heart becomes increasingly receptive to deeper encounters with the Eternal, recognizing patterns of goodness and relational love that point beyond the self.

The river of insight thus shapes understanding in ways that are both internal and external. It prepares the human spirit to recognize fullness when it arrives, offering guidance, moral courage, and reflective awareness as ongoing companions. Each moment of ethical awareness or philosophical recognition is a tributary that enriches the heart's capacity to perceive truth and participate in the moral and relational reality that is ultimately revealed in Christ.

12.3 The River of Relational Encounter

The river of relational encounter represents the culmination of the converging currents of human longing and insight. All the tributaries of desire for meaning, moral awareness, and ethical striving find their fulfillment in the living presence of Christ, who embodies truth, goodness, and love in a relational and accessible way. Human hearts, shaped by reflection, conscience, and spiritual aspiration, are drawn into a personal encounter where these longings are no longer abstract but tangible and transformative.

Relational imagery helps illuminate this convergence. Friendship illustrates mutual care and attentiveness, revealing how love and loyalty shape human life. Guidance reflects the reception of wisdom and moral clarity from a trusted source, showing that relational knowledge directs both ethical choices and personal growth. Acts of mercy and compassion demonstrate the reciprocity inherent in relational fulfillment, where one responds to the needs of others and, in doing so, participates in the ongoing flow of divine love. Personal transformation, whether in patience, humility, forgiveness, or courage, signals the heart's engagement with a presence that is both guiding and sustaining.

The human response to this relational encounter flows naturally from the convergence of longing and insight. Openness of heart allows awareness of the presence that has been preparing the soul throughout life. Trust emerges as reliance on the goodness, wisdom, and love that Christ embodies, enabling one to navigate moral and relational challenges with confidence and hope. Relational surrender does not imply weakness but reflects a conscious choice to participate in the life, light, and love that has been gradually revealed through ethical striving, devotional practice, and contemplative reflection.

Ordinary experiences, such as acts of care, moments of honest dialogue, or attentive listening, become avenues where the river of relational encounter is visible and active. In these encounters, the fullness of truth, moral goodness, and loving presence is not merely a concept but a lived reality. The heart recognizes that fulfillment is not an endpoint achieved by effort alone but a gift received through relational openness and trust. Through this convergence, human longing finds its answer, moral insight gains its direction, and ethical striving discovers its purpose in the relational presence that sustains, guides, and transforms.

12.4 Harmony in Daily Life

The convergence of human longing, insight, and relational encounter becomes visible in the rhythm of ordinary life, where ethical clarity, spiritual awareness, and loving engagement intertwine seamlessly. Moral decisions, once guided solely by duty or principle, take on a new depth when shaped by relational awareness and the presence of Christ. Choosing honesty in daily work, demonstrating fairness in interpersonal interactions, or standing for justice in challenging circumstances reflects the integration of ethical ideals with lived experience. Each choice embodies the flowing together of conscience, moral courage, and relational attentiveness.

Compassionate acts become another visible expression of this harmony. Offering help to those in need, forgiving those who have wronged us, and supporting the vulnerable are not abstract obligations but responses arising naturally from the awareness of relational presence. In these moments, the currents of longing and insight intersect with lived action, revealing that moral sensitivity and spiritual discernment translate into tangible love for others. Ethical integrity is no longer a separate pursuit from relational engagement; the two feed and strengthen each other in ordinary life.

Reflective moments further deepen this harmony. Pausing to consider one's choices, meditating on daily experiences, or silently attending to the inner movement of conscience allows the heart to perceive patterns of truth, goodness, and relational love in life. These moments illuminate the ways in which spiritual and ethical awareness, when embraced in practice, guide both small and significant decisions.

Relationships also provide a practical field where convergence manifests. Family, friends, and colleagues become mirrors of relational insight, offering opportunities to practice patience, empathy, and attentive listening. Loving engagement in these interactions reflects the internal harmony cultivated through ethical reflection and spiritual attentiveness.

In the daily flow of life, the integration of moral clarity, spiritual awareness, and relational responsiveness demonstrates that fulfillment is not an abstract ideal but a lived reality. The river of longing, insight, and encounter continues to shape ordinary life, making each decision, each act of care, and each reflective pause an expression of the harmony that emerges when human hearts are open to truth, goodness, and relational love.

12.5 Rivers Meeting the Ocean — Fulfillment in Christ

All the streams of human longing, ethical striving, and spiritual insight ultimately find their convergence in the relational presence of Christ, much like rivers flowing into the vastness of the ocean. The journey that began with quiet yearning, moral reflection, and intuitive awareness reaches its fullness in union with the Eternal. Christ embodies the fulfillment of truth, goodness, and love in a way that transforms both inner life and outward action. Recognition of this relational presence brings a profound sense of inner peace, where the restless currents of desire and doubt are met with assurance and harmony.

Engagement with this fullness cultivates moral courage. Actions once constrained by fear, uncertainty, or indecision are guided by a deeper clarity of conscience and relational awareness. Ethical choices become infused with love, patience, and empathy, reflecting the ongoing formation of character that arises naturally when the heart encounters Christ. Relationships gain new depth as acts of service, forgiveness, and care are rooted not only in obligation but in participatory love that mirrors the divine relational reality.

Spiritual growth is continuous, not static, and flows from the ongoing recognition and participation in the fullness already present. Meditation, reflection, and attentive living become ways to remain immersed in the currents of divine life, allowing the heart to perceive guidance, inspiration, and encouragement even in ordinary circumstances. Each day offers new opportunities to experience the integration of aspiration, ethical striving, and relational engagement, demonstrating that the ocean of fulfillment is not distant but present here and now.

Readers are invited to notice this fullness in their own lives, to recognize moments where peace, courage, and love emerge unexpectedly, and to participate actively in the living reality of Christ. The rivers that have flowed through longing, insight, and encounter meet the eternal ocean, offering both the completion of past yearnings and a dynamic path forward for continual growth in truth, goodness, and relational love.

Conclusion: Contemplating the Confluence

The convergence of human longing, ethical insight, and relational love invites a moment of attentive reflection. Each person can pause to consider where these currents meet in their own life, noticing the ways desire for truth, goodness, and intimacy with the Divine shape decisions, relationships, and moments of quiet awareness. There is space here for meditation, journaling, or prayerful contemplation, allowing the heart to trace the pathways of growth, moral courage, and relational openness that have emerged throughout life.

The image of rivers flowing together into a boundless ocean captures the richness of this encounter. Just as separate streams merge to form a vast, living body of water, the various aspects of human experience—yearning, striving, insight, and devotion—are unified in the relational fullness offered in Christ. This convergence brings harmony to the heart, deepens moral and spiritual awareness, and opens a horizon of hope, love, and ongoing transformation. In recognizing and participating in this confluence, the soul experiences a living reality that both fulfills the deepest longings and invites continual growth in truth, goodness, and relational presence.

Epilogue

The journey explored in this work traces the human heart from its earliest longings through moments of moral and spiritual insight, arriving at the fullness of relational encounter with Christ. Human life is marked by an innate yearning for truth, goodness, and love, which surfaces in conscience, ethical striving, and devotion. Across cultures, texts, and philosophical reflections, glimpses of the Eternal have appeared, offering guidance and awakening the heart, yet they remain partial and preparatory. These insights, whether experienced as moral ideals, devotional practices, or reflective awareness, all point toward a deeper fulfillment beyond what the human mind and spirit can fully attain on their own.

Christ emerges as the culmination of this journey, embodying the truth that the heart has sought, the goodness that inspires ethical life, and the relational love that heals and unites. The Gospels and relational witness portray a life lived in integrity, compassion, and mercy, illustrating that the Divine is not a distant ideal but an active presence in human experience. Encountering Christ invites trust, relational openness, and moral courage, enabling the heart to participate in a transformative life that integrates ethical discernment, spiritual insight, and relational love.

This relational presence carries both joy and renewal. Life in Christ illuminates moments of ordinary existence, transforming routine choices into reflections of truth and opportunities for love. The call is not toward mere ritual or abstract belief but toward active engagement, where ethical action, compassionate relationships, and reflective awareness become intertwined with the flow of divine life. Human experience, when attended to with reflection and openness, becomes a living testimony of light, love, and eternal truth.

Readers are invited to continue noticing these currents in their own lives. Reflect on the ways truth shapes decisions, goodness guides ethical engagement, and relational love fosters connection with others. Consider the moments when conscience, insight, and heart-longing converge, revealing the presence of the Eternal in daily experience. In this reflective journey, the invitation is to participate fully, cultivating moral awareness, relational sensitivity, and spiritual depth, recognizing that the fullness of life, light, and love is always offered, already present, and continually accessible.

The path traced throughout this book emphasizes that human longing is not an isolated condition but a guiding compass toward relational fulfillment. Glimpses of truth and goodness prepare the heart, ethical striving cultivates attentiveness, and devotional openness awakens relational receptivity. When these streams converge, the heart discovers Christ as the living reality that fulfills all yearning, revealing a life enriched with harmony, joy, and eternal significance. The journey continues in each moment, inviting the reader to live attentively, act compassionately, and love deeply, integrating the eternal triad of truth, goodness, and relational fullness into the ongoing story of their own life.

Appendices

Appendix A: Glossary of Key Sanskrit and Biblical Terms
This section provides concise definitions and context for terms frequently referenced in the text to aid comprehension and facilitate further study.

- **Ātman**: The innermost self or soul; in Hindu philosophy, the eternal essence of an individual.
- **Brahman**: Ultimate reality or universal spirit, representing the source and foundation of all existence.
- **Bhakti**: Devotional love or devotion directed toward God or a personal deity, emphasizing relational intimacy.
- **Dharma**: Duty, moral order, and ethical responsibility guiding human conduct.
- **Ahimsa**: Principle of nonviolence in thought, word, and action.
- **Satya**: Truth or fidelity to ultimate reality and moral principles.
- **Ṛta**: Cosmic order or the principle of natural law governing the universe in Vedic thought.
- **Logos**: Term from John 1:1 representing the Word, divine reason, and relational expression of God in the world.
- **Grace**: Unmerited favor or relational generosity from God, enabling moral and spiritual transformation.
- **Eternal Life**: Participation in divine life, relational union with God, and fulfillment of human longing.

Appendix B: Parallel Text References

This section highlights correspondences between key passages in Hindu scriptures and the Bible that illustrate ethical ideals, devotional orientation, and spiritual insight.

Theme	Vedas / Upanishads / Gita	Bible
Ultimate Reality	Chandogya Upanishad 6.8: Ātman and Brahman	John 1:1–5: The Word as source of life
Ethical Living	Bhagavad Gita 3.19: Perform duty without attachment	Micah 6:8: Act justly, love mercy, walk humbly
Devotional Love	Bhakti poems of Mirabai and Surdas	John 13:34–35: Love one another as I have loved you
Moral Courage	Mahabharata narratives of ethical choice	Joshua 1:9: Be strong and courageous
Guidance & Protection	Gita 4.7–8: Divine intervention to restore dharma	Psalm 23: God as shepherd and protector
Forgiveness	Stories of penance and reconciliation in Puranas	Luke 15: Parable of the Prodigal Son
Spiritual Insight	Upanishadic meditation on Brahman	James 1:5: Seek wisdom from God

Appendix C: Suggested Readings for Deeper Study

This section lists accessible primary texts, translations, and scholarly resources for readers who wish to explore ethical, devotional, and philosophical themes more deeply.

Hindu Scriptures and Commentaries
- Rig Veda, trans. Wendy Doniger
- Bhagavad Gita, trans. Eknath Easwaran
- Upanishads, trans. Patrick Olivelle
- Selected Bhakti poetry of Mirabai, Surdas, and Tulsidas

Biblical Texts and Commentaries
- Holy Bible, English Standard Version (KJV) or New Revised Standard Version (NRSV)
- John, the Gospel according to John
- Pauline Epistles, especially Romans and Corinthians
- Matthew, particularly the Sermon on the Mount

Other Books by the Author, Dr. Venkat Potana
https://www.amazon.com/author/venkat19

	Shot Title of the Book	Amazon link
1	Chains of Anxiety	https://www.amazon.com/dp/B0FQ31LJL6
2	Theology of Sickness	https://www.amazon.com/dp/B0FPXQJ8PR
3	Echoes of the Call	https://www.amazon.com/dp/B0FB3WH3W5
4	Multiplying Disciples	https://www.amazon.com/dp/B0FJGBLC4Y
5	Time Traveler of the Soul	https://www.amazon.com/dp/B0FKSZXPZX
6	History of Christianity in AP	https://www.amazon.com/dp/B0FPBDT5PW
7	Ten Christian Doctrines	https://www.amazon.com/dp/B0FPD45X75
8	Campus Ministry	https://www.amazon.com/dp/B0D7S5XVJ2
9	Witnessing to Tribals	https://www.amazon.com/dp/B0DCVXBP1J
10	Desperation to Deliverance	https://www.amazon.com/dp/B0FCMTCR9C
11	Shadows Of The Street	https://www.amazon.com/dp/B0DK7LVGGV
12	Old Testament Themes	https://www.amazon.com/dp/B0DB7FLJBJ
13	Missiological Themes; Vol-1	https://www.amazon.com/dp/B0F9495K6M
14	Missiological Themes; Vol-2	https://www.amazon.com/dp/B0D5VRBD8M
15	Hand in Hand with God	https://www.amazon.com/dp/B0FF2NK2F9
16	From Fever to Freedom	https://www.amazon.com/dp/B0FCMY5B7P
17	The Compassionate Healer	https://www.amazon.com/dp/B0FDLBGWGP
18	Power and Provision	https://www.amazon.com/dp/B0F6D3GJZP
19	Becoming Like Christ	https://www.amazon.com/dp/B0F8HB3LW5
20	Migrants in God's Mission	https://www.amazon.com/dp/B0F9XB2WV5
21	Grace-Filled Parenting	https://www.amazon.com/dp/B0DS1LVRSP
22	The Preacher's Tool	https://www.amazon.com/dp/B0F32KJFZ6
23	Missions Historiography	https://www.amazon.com/dp/B0D578MPN5
24	Grace-Filled Marriage	https://www.amazon.com/dp/B0DWLJB8Y1
25	Echoes of Eternity	https://www.amazon.com/dp/B0DHPGGZG8
26	Tribals in India	https://www.amazon.com/dp/B0D98FZTVY
27	New Testament Themes	https://www.amazon.com/dp/B0DJBZ9HTD
28	Indigenous Missions	https://www.amazon.com/dp/B0DKTNY555
29	Shadows Of The Street	https://www.amazon.com/dp/B0D6GYHRR9
30	Theological Themes	https://www.amazon.com/dp/B0D683CMTD
31	A Theological Response to Street Children	https://www.amazon.com/Theological-Response-Street-Children-Empirical/dp/9351480534
32	Witnessing to Students	https://www.amazon.com/Witnessing-Students-Efficacy-UESI-India
33	Indigenous Missions in Post-Independent India- An Empirical Study	https://www.christianworldimprints.com/index.php?p=sr&Uc=7732643155826867191
34	Overcoming Depression	https://www.amazon.com/dp/B0FQ468J25
35	Gospel Movements in India	https://www.amazon.com/dp/B0FQ49M1T2
36	Overcoming Pornography	https://www.amazon.com/dp/B0FQCQFMNJ
36	Sex Addiction	https://www.amazon.com/dp/B0FQNCPMW1
37	Overcoming Suicidal Tendency	https://www.amazon.com/dp/B0FQTQZXMN

38	History of Christianity in Karnataka	https://www.amazon.com/dp/B0FT8X3QV9
39	*Quiet Time*	https://www.amazon.com/dp/B0FTFPKH9Q
40	Hinduism Through Bhakta's Eyes	https://www.amazon.com/dp/B0FTXYY8TP
41	365 Days of Daily Devotions	https://www.amazon.com/dp/B0FVG1W4D4
42	నిజమైన మోక్షం: కర్మ నుండి కృప వరకు ఒక ప్రయాణం	https://store.pothi.com/book/డాక్టర్-వెంకట్-పోతన-నిజమైన-మోక్షం-కర్మ-నుండి-కృప-వరకు-ఒక-ప్రయాణం
43	ఆత్మయానం: జ్ఞాపకాల తీరాలకు తిరుగు ప్రయాణం	https://store.pothi.com/book/డా-వెంకట్-పోతన-ఆత్మయానం-జ్ఞాపకాల-తీరాలకు-తిరుగు-ప్రయాణం
44	Satyam, Shivam, Christam	

Other Books by the Author, Dr. Venkat Potana
Indian readers can purchase @ Pothi.com

	Shot Title of the Book	Amazon link
1	Chains of Anxiety	https://www.amazon.com/dp/B0FQ31LJL6
2	Theology of Sickness	https://www.amazon.com/dp/B0FPXQJ8PR
3	Echoes of the Call	https://www.amazon.com/dp/B0FB3WH3W5
4	Multiplying Disciples	https://www.amazon.com/dp/B0FJGBLC4Y
5	Time Traveler of the Soul	https://www.amazon.com/dp/B0FKSZXPZX
6	History of Christianity in AP	https://www.amazon.com/dp/B0FPBDT5PW
7	Ten Christian Doctrines	https://www.amazon.com/dp/B0FPD45X75
8	Campus Ministry	https://www.amazon.com/dp/B0D7S5XVJ2
9	Witnessing to Tribals	https://www.amazon.com/dp/B0DCVXBP1J
10	Desperation to Deliverance	https://www.amazon.com/dp/B0FCMTCR9C
11	Shadows Of The Street	https://www.amazon.com/dp/B0DK7LVGGV
12	Old Testament Themes	https://www.amazon.com/dp/B0DB7FLJBJ
13	Missiological Themes; Vol-1	https://www.amazon.com/dp/B0F9495K6M
14	Missiological Themes; Vol-2	https://www.amazon.com/dp/B0D5VRBD8M
15	Hand in Hand with God	https://www.amazon.com/dp/B0FF2NK2F9
16	From Fever to Freedom	https://www.amazon.com/dp/B0FCMY5B7P
17	The Compassionate Healer	https://www.amazon.com/dp/B0FDLBGWGP
18	Power and Provision	https://www.amazon.com/dp/B0F6D3GJZP
19	Becoming Like Christ	https://www.amazon.com/dp/B0F8HB3LW5
20	Migrants in God's Mission	https://www.amazon.com/dp/B0F9XB2WV5
21	Grace-Filled Parenting	https://www.amazon.com/dp/B0DS1LVRSP
22	The Preacher's Tool	https://www.amazon.com/dp/B0F32KJFZ6
23	Missions Historiography	https://www.amazon.com/dp/B0D578MPN5
24	Grace-Filled Marriage	https://www.amazon.com/dp/B0DWLJB8Y1
25	Echoes of Eternity	https://www.amazon.com/dp/B0DHPGGZG8
26	Tribals in India	https://www.amazon.com/dp/B0D98FZTVY
27	New Testament Themes	https://www.amazon.com/dp/B0DJBZ9HTD
28	Indigenous Missions	https://www.amazon.com/dp/B0DKTNY555
29	Shadows Of The Street	https://www.amazon.com/dp/B0D6GYHRR9
30	Theological Themes	https://www.amazon.com/dp/B0D683CMTD
31	A Theological Response to Street Children	https://www.amazon.com/Theological-Response-Street-Children-Empirical/dp/9351480534
32	Witnessing to Students	https://www.amazon.com/Witnessing-Students-Efficacy-UESI-India
33	Indigenous Missions in Post-Independent India- An Empirical Study	https://www.christianworldimprints.com/index.php?p=sr&Uc=7732643155826867191
34	Overcoming Depression	https://www.amazon.com/dp/B0FQ468J25
35	*Gospel Movements in India*	https://www.amazon.com/dp/B0FQ49M1T2
36	Overcoming Pornography	https://www.amazon.com/dp/B0FQCQFMNJ
36	Sex Addiction	https://www.amazon.com/dp/B0FQNCPMW1
37	Overcoming Suicidal Tendency	https://www.amazon.com/dp/B0FQTQZXMN

38	History of Christianity in Karnataka	https://www.amazon.com/dp/B0FT8X3QV9
39	*Quiet Time*	https://www.amazon.com/dp/B0FTFPKH9Q
40	Hinduism Through Bhakta's Eyes	https://www.amazon.com/dp/B0FTXYY8TP
41	365 Days of Daily Devotions	https://www.amazon.com/dp/B0FVG1W4D4
42	నిజమైన మోక్షం: కర్మ నుండి కృప వరకు ఒక ప్రయాణం	https://store.pothi.com/book/డాక్టర్-వెంకట్-పోతన-నిజమైన-మోక్షం-కర్మ-నుండి-కృప-వరకు-ఒక-ప్రయాణం
43	ఆత్మయానం: జ్ఞాపకాల తీరాలకు తిరుగు ప్రయాణం	https://store.pothi.com/book/డా-వెంకట్-పోతన-ఆత్మయానం-జ్ఞాపకాల-తీరాలకు-తిరుగు-ప్రయాణం
44	Satyam, Shivam, Christam	

Note to Readers
Indian readers can purchase all these books directly from Pothi.com. Buying through international platforms such as Amazon.com may be costly due to currency conversion and shipping charges. The author has published the works in India through Pothi.com for easier and more affordable access. Simply visit Pothi.com, type the title of the book in the search bar, and place your order online.

Made in the USA
Coppell, TX
20 February 2026

71902046R00085